What pe
about *Soft Skill*

Learning NALED has fundamentally changed the way I lead. It opened me up and made me question my internal behaviours, and the way I behaved with my team. Applying it has helped me open up and be more curious, and helped me stop shooting people down.

I used to say the right things, do everything I was asked but be physically and emotionally distant. People sensed a lack of engagement from me. I now have better, more personal connection with my team and peers, which is creating deeper trust and being more productive.

Rob, IT

I can't begin to tell you what a difference using NALED has already made in my world. I've been using it in my conversations at work and it has thrown up some underlying tensions and issues that I was not yet aware of. On top of that I personally feel more involved with each of those people, so I am motivated to make changes to help them. I'm noticing a difference both in me and with the information level I am receiving.

Janet, Operations

These aren't just soft skills; they are life skills. My daughter called in a panic to say her boyfriend was dealing with a major home issue. I told her to bring him here. Prior to learning about NALED, I would have probably told him to 'man up' and gone for a beer. Instead I sat with him and listened. I heard him whilst he cried, I acknowledged his situation and just listened. After an hour and a half you could see his shoulders drop and his face clear. It made a real difference in his life. My wife and daughter were surprised and proud of me too.

Phil, Director

I practised this recently in a meeting with a group of stakeholders who were unhappy about the project and where it's at. Instead of arguing the points with them as I would have usually done, I held a listening forum. I heard what they had to say. This has resulted in better conversations and them being more bought into what we are trying to achieve and why.

Jared, Major Projects

NALED really resonated with me as a GP of many years. I've realized this is what I do in my successful consultations with patients. I have evolved my style over the years as I unconsciously recognized that if I don't approach my patients in this way, the consultation will fail, and I am much more likely to miss both the patient's agenda and important information to aid diagnosis. Now I have the explicit framework I can be more conscious about it.

Dr Collier, GP

I have just started in a new team and have been using the NALED techniques to be more intentional; focusing, listening and asking careful questions. It is drawing more information out of people, resulting in better preparation for the meetings. I am getting the information I need for my reports in the meeting rather than having to chase people afterwards, so it is making my life easier and making me more respected and effective in role.

Christine, Maintenance

The main impact on me has been my awareness of my own reaction to people around me. I've learnt not to pre-judge problems as they walk through the door. I'm now aware and conscious that I've done that in the past. Learning NALED has has helped me allow people to open up first.

Mary, Security

At home I have had a situation with my best friend. He's always been life and soul of the party – very different to me. But he told me last week that he is suffering from depression. Badly. NALED has given me a way of handling my own deep emotions and a way of holding a caring, compassionate conversation with him. He's got a long way to go, but he knows I am on his side and have the ability to just shut up and listen. This is life-changing stuff.

Paul, Major Projects

In my work as an engineer, it is amazing how infrequently different departments talk to each other to resolve joint issues. I end up getting praised for 'pulling the teams together' by simply holding NALED conversations. It shouldn't be that easy to get praise, but when no one else does it, then it seems like a big deal.

Gary, Engineering

I am trying to use NALED on a regular basis. I am finding that the more I try to empower the team, the better the team responds and the more effectively we are delivering for the customer. I am also working my way through my social capital map, trying to ensure those connections are maintained and improved.

Mark, Director

Just because we go to work, it doesn't mean we all switch our emotions off and become machines. If we're going to truly make a change, we have to remember that a business is a complex mechanism – it's organic, it relies on people – sometimes even the seemingly irrational. But focusing on people is essential to delivering the needed change. NALED has given me the 'how' to do this.

Steve, Systems

In progress meetings, instead of telling people what they should be doing, I now ask my team what they are going to do next and Notice, Acknowledge and Listen to their response. It is less work for me and results in better engagement.

Michelle, Construction

I would love to hear your stories too, do share them with me at lucy@naled.org

LUCY HARRISON

SOFT SKILLS FOR TOUGH JOBS

Building teams that WORK,
one conversation at a time

The illustrations are by Bekah Funning.
NALED is a registered Trademark.

First published in Great Britain by Practical Inspiration Publishing, 2022

The moral rights of the author have been asserted

ISBN   9781788603485   (print)
        9781788603508   (epub)
        9781788603492   (mobi)

Every effort has been made to trace copyright holders and to obtain their permission for the use of copyright material. The publisher apologizes for any errors or omissions and would be grateful if notified of any corrections that should be incorporated in future reprints or editions of this book.

Want to bulk-buy copies of this book for your team and colleagues? We can introduce case studies, customize the content and co-brand *Soft Skills for Tough Jobs* to suit your business's needs.

Please email info@practicalinspiration.com for more details.

Soft skills are a dark art,
but one you are already using.
Learn how to get better.

Contents

Acknowledgements ....*xiii*

Foreword .... *xv*

1. **Introduction** 1
    How to use this book... 10

2. **The five strands of NALED – an overview** 13
    The three principles of practice 19
    Summary 21

3. **Notice**.. 23
    The problem: What you notice is not all there is –
        but you may believe it is... 26
    The solution: Notice intentionally................................... 27
    How do you become more effective at noticing? 30
    What to watch out for 48
    Notice summary 51

4. **Acknowledge** 53
    The problem: We pretend not to notice...................................... 56
    The solution: Acknowledge the good, the bad
        and the ugly.. 57
    How do you acknowledge? 61
    What to watch out for 75
    Acknowledge summary.. 79

5. **Listen** **81**
The problem: Your listening is driven by your
own agenda 84
The solution: Get off your agenda and give people a
darn good listening to 86
How do you listen more effectively? 91
Listen summary 107

5½. **STOP and practise** **109**
The natural break 110
What to watch out for 112

6. **Explore** **115**
The problem: You jump into solutions mode 117
The solution: Slow down and develop a systematic
approach to problem solving 120
How to explore 122
Exploring with others 130
Exploring your situation 134
Explore summary 140

7. **Do** **143**
The problem: You often don't do 145
The solution: Create the case for action 148
How do you move to Do? 151
What to watch out for 158
Do summary 159

8. **Applying NALED in a nutshell** **161**
Choice 1 – Choose to have a different kind of
conversation 164
Choice 2 – Choose to show up and respond differently 167
Choice 3 – Choose to see the world differently 171
Summary 175

8½. STOP and reflect **177**
    Questionnaire: How good are your soft skills? 178
    Reflection: How good are your relationships? 182

9.   Challenges you might face **185**
    What about when the conversations get tough? 186
    What about when my buttons have been pushed? 189
    How do I turn down the level of emotion? 190
    What else should I look out for? 191
    The benefits of support networks – who do you
       talk with? 196
    Next steps 196

10. Stories from the front line **199**
    Group stories 200
    Final thoughts 205

Bibliography *209*

Index *213*

Acknowledgements

This book would never have happened without the belief and the generous support of a whole raft of people.

Colin, without you I wouldn't have started on this journey in the first place; thank you.

Judy, thank you for persuading me to write the book of NALED. Kerry, your enthusiasm gave me motivation when I needed it most.

Jo C., your coaching helped me shape it into something worth reading.

Jo T., Steve Y., Rob M., Alina N., and Mark T.; all of you generously gave your time to help shape the final version. Thank you.

Then to the team who made it all become real:

- Bekah, for creating illustrations that make me smile, thank you for understanding.
- Sally, for taking me away from it all and letting me burble, thank you for listening.
- Alison and the Practical Inspiration team, thank you for sculpting the final manuscript.

And, of course, Rob Funning. You have challenged, refined and focused my thinking every step of the way. Thank you for your generous, heartfelt and thoughtful help; *Soft Skills for Tough Jobs* is better because of you.

Finally, a big thank you to my family for supporting me along the way and testing me continuously. I am not sure you intended to help me learn, but you have.

Foreword

Soft Skills for Tough Jobs is a book for everyone who wants to be a great leader, a great colleague or a great friend. Ideally, you might want to be all three!

Borne of deeply personal experiences and professional encounters, Lucy Harrison offers a compelling perspective that all our lives can be enhanced by improving the quality of our conversations. That's easy to say, but hard to do, right?

She introduces a new and simple framework to help us do just that. Her NALED framework is all about building on what we do well already, and developing the habits that will help us excel. She backs it up with practical exercises, stories that show it in action, and points to great free resources for taking it further. And to help us remember it all she uses simple graphics that really stick.

Let's face it, the world would be a far better place if we could all communicate better, and learning from a great book seems the least we can do to play our part.

Some books take a lot of reading; they get put to one side several times because they seem just too hard, or worse, they go left unfinished altogether. I doubt this will happen with this book. I read it in one sitting and have gone back to it several times when planning a challenging conversation.

Adrienne Kelbie, CBE

Chapter 1
Introduction

Collaboration: working jointly with
others or together for common purpose,
cooperating with others to achieve or do
something; partnership or teamwork.

I've always been a do-er. One of life's problem solvers.

I learned how to solve my own problems as they occurred as a result of growing up and working on farms. My early career in corporate events taught me how to solve other people's problems quickly and effectively.

It was when I moved into the outdoor industry, leading team and leadership development projects, that I learned how to pre-empt problems and solve them before they could occur.

I was good at it.

But one day came a problem I couldn't solve. What I learned from it shaped my professional relationships, my career and this book.

My husband is a paramedic, the kind of problem solver you really want around when life goes pear-shaped.

He has emotional moments when he comes home at the end of shifts. It is part of the job; he sees people at their worst. But he began to become more unpredictable. I didn't know what would come through the door at the end of a shift. It became a problem.

I tried to solve it.

'Why don't you go for a run, love?' I'd suggest, 'I often find it helpful to get my emotions out and release some endorphins.'

'You look like you could do with some time out. Would you like me to take the kids away for a day or so?'

Or:

'Have you thought about going to the doctor? Some people find that medication/therapy/counselling (delete as appropriate) really helps.'

It didn't help.

In fact, the more I tried to solve it, fix it, rescue him, the worse it became.

By trying to solve his problems for him, it implied that he couldn't do it himself; that he was not capable. He then felt rubbish that he couldn't fix it himself, beat himself up further and spiralled downwards. He felt disempowered.

On top of that, it also implied that I was somehow better than him, someone with answers where he had none. He felt incompetent.

He couldn't see a way forward when he really wanted to. He felt frustrated. All this on top of the mental health issue that had arisen.

We argued. A lot. It usually ended up with me suggesting he needed to change; that I was right, he was wrong.

Our relationship got worse.

Of course, the kids got the flack. They became reactive and overwrought. I tried to fix them too. That didn't work either.

I was stressed, pressured and wanted to help, but I realized that what I was doing wasn't helping; that something had to change, and that the only thing I had the power to change was me. I noticed my behaviour and I acknowledged that I was part of the problem. If I kept doing what I was doing, there was only one way this relationship was going to go.

So, I shut up.

I stopped trying to fix it. Instead, I noticed *him*, I acknowledged *him* and I listened to *him*. It was really hard. I had to bite my tongue, sit on my hands, pinch myself, stay still...

Eventually, he started to open up. He started to talk and, still, I just listened (I say 'just', but at the time I didn't realize quite how difficult and yet how powerful this can be). It took some weeks. It took my stillness, my attention, my belief that he could do this for himself. In time he turned a corner. He realized he had a deeper problem and sought some professional help.

Instead of finding a solution for him, I let him find his own. Over time, our relationship improved, our family life improved and my career improved as I started to apply this in other areas.

'I learned how my change in approach to the situation ended up changing the situation itself.'

I share this story because it was the catalyst for my own journey. I learned how my *change in approach* to the situation (how I showed up, my response and my thinking) ended up changing the situation itself. I learned these soft skills in a tough situation.

I'd worked in team and leadership development for many years, but this experience led me to research and train to learn more. I studied and practised to become a professional coach. In the years since this story occurred, I have worked with and listened to many individuals and teams.

I've discovered the difference in the outcomes of a conversation when I approach it as 'Lucy's hardwired reactions' to when I approach it as 'Lucy's intentional response'.

The simple truth is that my approach to a conversation affects the results in that relationship.

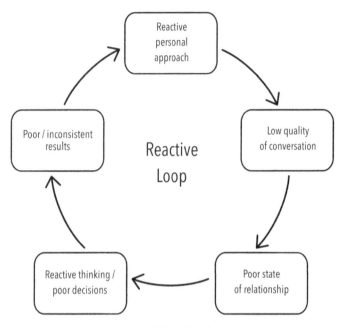

Figure 1 Reactive Loop

In the story outlined, I had been locked in the Reactive Loop. My approach was on autopilot and I was reacting according to usual patterns. These reactions led to a low quality of conversation. Poor conversations impacted on the state of our relationship, which in turn led to reactive thinking and poor decisions that, of course, gave us poor or inconsistent results, which made me react more… and so on.

When I changed my approach, I moved into the Intentional Loop. One conversation at a time, I became more intentionally present for him, concerned more about the long-term outcome than fixing the immediate issue. My presence improved the depth and quality of our conversation, result-ing in a more positive relationship. This in turn gave us the space to think more effectively and make decisions that improved the situation. The better results meant I was less frustrated, so had more wherewithal to continue to approach the conversation differently.

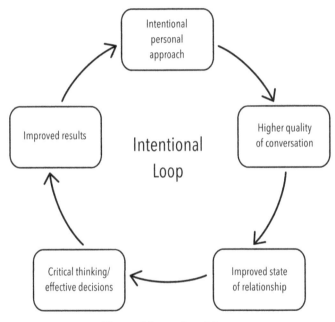

Figure 2 Intentional Loop

The more I examined these two loops, combining the inten-tional and coaching approaches, the more I noticed there were common threads weaving together in all the best con-versations, in all the best strategic thinking, in all the best team relationships.

Over the course of ten years of experience and practice, I honed these threads into this coherent framework that I am now introducing to you – NALED: Notice, Acknowledge, Listen, Explore, Do (pronounced 'nailed').

The NALED framework is a simple and effective way for you to improve the results of your interactions with others.

I've now introduced NALED to many hundreds of business leaders, who in turn have used it and taught it to others. It works.

It works because it is based around what you *already do* when you are at your best. The best conversations you have, the best chats, the best relationships, the best strategic thinking, the best collaborations.

As you become more intentional about your approach, you can be your best more often.

> *'As you become more intentional*
> *about your approach, you can be*
> *your best more often.'*

This intentional approach works because it gives you choice:

- The choice to show up differently; to choose your approach to a situation or person;
- The choice and skills to hold a different kind of conversation or interaction; and
- The choice to respond rather than react to unfolding circumstances.

Together these choices will change how your conversations play out. People will become more engaged. Your relationships will improve. Teams will become more collaborative.

Getting beyond the usual chat is a way of giving you choice in those moments when it matters.

As you've picked this book up, you are probably already aware that the so-called 'soft' skills of relationships, communication, influence and engagement are essential to effective team collaboration, improved decision making and sustained productivity. You are probably also aware that they are some of the hardest things to get right. What works with one person or one team, in one situation, may not work in another.

Your workplace may be tough, the projects may be physical, technical, life threatening or highly regulated. It may be that your industry is traditionally not used to considering emotions, wellbeing or relationships. You may be worried that if you start getting all 'fluffy' then you'll get laughed at, pushed aside, ignored.

If this is you, you are not alone. I have been working with people like you all my working life. This approach will work.

The NALED framework I will introduce is a practical, pragmatic way of approaching soft skills. That's not to say it's going to be easy; changing ingrained habits never is. The initial effort to do something differently may be tricky, but using this framework will make your life easier and possibly even more fulfilling in the long run.

By using the NALED framework, you can intentionally choose how you interact with people and situations and, more importantly, know how to improve them.

You can get beyond the usual chat to strengthen relationships and improve teamwork.

How to use this book

This book is designed to be something you can easily read in one sitting or dip in and out of when you need it. Each chapter has stories and exercises so you can develop your understanding and skills, and there are additional resources available on the website www.naled.org

In Chapter 2, I'll introduce you to the framework, NALED (Notice, Acknowledge, Listen, Explore, Do) as a whole.

I will then go through each strand in detail in the following chapters, using exercises, top tips and stories to help you focus on each area in turn, before running through some of the common challenges you might encounter along the way.

Chapter 8 gives you quick, actionable ways of applying the whole framework. You'll have a chance to reflect and evaluate so you can see where best to apply what you've learned.

It would be wrong of me to pretend that working with people is simple, so Chapter 9 introduces some challenges you may face and things to watch out for.

Finally, I'll share stories from other people of how they've applied the framework and the impact they've had.

Remember, **NALED is what you are already doing**. Even being conscious of it will already make you more effective. The more you use it, the better you will get. You will build relationships and teams that are more effective with every conversation you hold.

You will develop soft skills that make tough jobs easier.

Chapter 2
The five strands of NALED:
An overview

Relationship: the way in which two or more people, groups, countries etc., talk to, behave towards, are connected to, and deal with each other.

In the story introduced in the last chapter, there were three things getting in the way of me having a helpful conversation. The first was me: I was getting in my own way because I wanted to fix it for my husband. The second was him: he was getting in the way because he was stuck and felt disempowered. The third was the situation: it was getting in the way because there was so much else going on. We had a young family and a relationship and lives to live at the same time.

These three areas, *Self*, *Other* and *Situation* (or SOS), are interconnected in our conversations and relationships. They are inextricably linked.

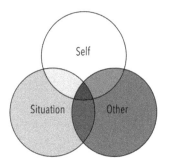

If you want to improve your engagement, conversations and relationships with each other, you must be aware of these three areas:

Figure 3 SOS: the interconnectedness of Self, Other and Situation

- *Self*: to become more *self-aware* and therefore be better able to self-manage.
- *Other*: to become more *socially aware*, and therefore better able to manage relationships.
- *Situation*: to become more *situationally aware*, and therefore better able to problem solve, plan and make effective decisions.

As I go through these strands and the framework as a whole, I will outline how it applies in each of these different areas.

The five strands of NALED

NALED: Notice, Acknowledge, Listen, Explore, Do

These are the five strands of the framework that you can weave together to make your conversations and interactions more effective.

- Notice: To pay attention to yourself, the other and the environment.
- Acknowledge: To bring what you notice to the table so you can choose to do something about it.
- Listen: To listen effectively and actively.
- Explore: To stay curious about the problem and get creative about solutions.
- Do: To decide the next steps, commit and act.

Think about a good conversation you have had recently. One that really made a difference. Take a step back and think about how the conversation proceeded. What did you Notice, Acknowledge, Listen to, Explore and Do? You will probably find that you were applying some, if not all, of this framework.

The shift in your effectiveness will come from being more intentional about using it. And yet NALED is not a step-by-step formula for success, but strands that you individually weave for different people and different situations. Apply the five strands as feels right to you at the time.

People are complex. Every one of us is different; interactions between two people are rarely similar. Throw more people into the mix with the changing world in which we live and work and the interaction possibilities are endless.

Here is a little more about each strand. Each is simple yet can also be incredibly hard. Our ingrained habits, biases[1] and desires get in the way, such as wanting to have a laugh, solve problems, be right... You can weave them in to improve your interactions and soft skills.

 ## Strand 1: NOTICE

See more of what you focus on. When you widen your lenses and actively seek to Notice more, you get more information and can make better decisions.

Use SOS – Notice *Self*, notice *Other(s)* and notice the *Situation*.

- By noticing your*self*, you look at what is going on in your personal world – the emotions or thoughts or pre-existing judgements you bring. Are these useful or not? How are you showing up to this conversation?
- By noticing the *other*, you seek to observe others' reactions, emotions, patterns and be curious about them. You thus demonstrate that you care about them.

---

[1]   See 'Examples of common cognitive bias' in Chapter 6.

- By noticing the *situation*, you see what impact the circumstances, environment, organizational or team culture and history have on the situation you are in right now.

 ## Strand 2: ACKNOWLEDGE

By acknowledging something, we bring it into the field of play or bring it to the table. Again, use SOS. Acknowledge *Self*, *Other(s)* and the *Situation*.

- Acknowledge what impact you might be having here. Is it helping?
- Acknowledge the *other* person and what you've noticed. This actively demonstrates that you care about them and hear them as a person.
- Acknowledge the *situation* as it is right now. You don't have to like it, but it is what it is.

 ## Strand 3: LISTEN

Listen actively and wholeheartedly to the other.

- Listening is the foundation of relationships. Listen to understand, to hear, with curiosity and an open mind. It is so hard to actively listen and shut yourself up, but this is the core of the approach – let the other person do the thinking and listen to them as they open up.
- Loop back. What are you Noticing? What do you need to Acknowledge?

- Be curious about what you are hearing; ask questions to hear more.

NAL is the core of this framework. Even if you only do NAL, it will still improve your relationships and the depth of your conversation with someone. Use NAL to de-escalate, to understand and to build trust.

I recommend staying with just NAL for a while as you learn the framework before moving on to E and D.

 **Strand 4: EXPLORE**

This is where you begin to seek opportunity and open up possibilities. Explore the facets of the problem and the potential solutions.

- As you introduce this strand, cycle back round to Notice, Acknowledge and Listen to everyone's response to the ideas (including your own). Let them do the thinking.
- Actively seek diverse opinions and mine for conflict to unlock thinking.

 **Strand 5: DO**

Make a decision, commit to the next steps and take action.

- Consider what is possible, what is likely and what might need more time or information.

- What will help make the decision more likely to happen?
- Be courageous.

Figure 4 The five strands of NALED woven together

The three principles of practice

Here are the three principles of applying NALED

1. Enjoy the messiness

I've mentioned already that this is not a process: you don't do N then A then L then E then D. We are dealing with communication and relationships and trust and rapport – people don't work like that. If it did, we would be robots and we would all have perfect relationships all around us.

NALED is messy because people are messy. You start with one strand and introduce another. You weave in the next and

circle around these for a while. You may introduce another for a while then take it away again. You might get to D and think you've finished, while instead you are right back at the beginning again.

Don't let this put you off; instead, let this joyful messiness of humanity inspire you to enjoy it – to embrace that we are not perfect but are all continuing to learn each day and trying to be a little bit better.

2. Be authentic

NALED is not a plaster or Sellotape. You can't just apply it willy-nilly as a 'tool' to fix something. It must be real, to come from the heart. You must honestly want to make a difference and really, truly care. If not, this will come across as manipulative and as 'management speak' and may have the opposite effect to the one you wish for.

So, if you are not bothered about improving relationships, about making your life easier by improving your approach to people, then I suggest you put the book down now.

3. Take small steps

Take it one step at a time. Try one thing differently and see how it goes. I'll introduce the strands in a linear fashion, but you don't have to apply NALED in that way. Feedback from one of our programmes recently said:

'It's small steps but it's leading big changes.'

And that's the point. If you read this whole book and try to be more intentional with every conversation you have, it is likely to feel too hard, too much, too overwhelming.

I am still learning day by day more about how to use NALED and be more effective in my approach to people. I may have identified the framework but it doesn't mean I'm perfect at it. Quite the opposite; I mess up regularly.

So, focus on small steps, tiny little changes, and make the small change a new habit.

In the next chapter, I will go into the strands in more detail, talking about the skills and techniques, providing some top tips, things that get in the way and exercises to help you learn. You can drop in and out; use as much or as little as you like. Try one bit and come back for a little more.

You can do this, one conversation at a time.

Summary

- ✓ It helps to be aware of the three elements of *Self*, *Other* and *Situation* as you seek to improve your soft skills.
- ✓ The five strands of NALED are Notice, Acknowledge, Listen, Explore and Do. Learn how to weave them together more effectively.

- ✓ The three principles of applying the NALED frame-work are:
  - ➢ Enjoy the messiness;
  - ➢ Be authentic; and
  - ➢ Take small steps.

CHAPTER THREE

Notice

Notice: the act of perceiving or observation, to pay attention to, to become conscious or aware of, respectful consideration, detection.

It was a busy A&E department late on a Sunday night. The paramedics brought in a woman with bad stomach pain, resulting in collapse and shifting consciousness. When the doctor questioned her, she blamed having eaten some dodgy food, to which her husband quietly countered, 'I ate the same sandwich; we shared it half each. I am fine. It must be something else.'

The patient was moved through into the 'crash' area to be given IV fluids, yet her blood pressure and oxygen saturation continued to drop.

There was a shift change in the early hours of the morning. The new doctor asked the same questions and got the same answers. Dodgy sandwich. The husband quietly saying 'no, I ate the same one; it must be something else.' The new doctor decided: 'Gastro-enteritis from dodgy food; we'll wait until the team get in later this morning.'

Other, louder patients came in. The woman got quieter, paler, colder. The husband worried but quietly trusted the system.

Finally, it was just too much for him. A nurse came to try and move her onto a ward. The husband argued. The senior consultant walked past, heard the argument, took one look at the woman on the bed and knew she was dying.

Then the team moved fast. It was not a stomach upset but an ectopic pregnancy that had ruptured. She was indeed very close to dying from internal blood loss.

When the incident was later studied, it transpired that the second doctor had been caught in traffic, late to work and missed the handover. The doctor was busy, distracted and listened to the woman, not her quieter husband. What he heard backed up his initial thoughts and he didn't Notice any dissenting voices or evidence.

That woman was me. After an emergency operation and a long recovery, I had my first child two years later.

The A&E department apologized profusely and now have set a new standard procedure in the department. A woman of child-bearing age showing my symptoms is now treated as an ectopic pregnancy first. A happy outcome that could easily have been tragic.

Doctors are human, and as such make mistakes. This story is not to blame, but a demonstration of how important it is to consciously Notice more.

'What you notice is not all there is;
but you may believe it is.'

The problem: What you notice is not all there is – but you may believe it is

A quick challenge for you. Count how many Fs there are in the following sentence. Take your time but only count once.

'Finished files are the result of years of scientific
study combined with the experience of years.'

What number did you come up with?

There are six Fs in this sentence. Most people see only three. There could be many reasons for this. Maybe they are reading it aloud in their heads and listening for the 'Eff' sound not the 'v' sound from the word 'Of', or maybe we just overlook the common words.

My kids play games to pass the time when on long car journeys. One of these is quite simply known as 'yellow car'. The rules are simple: the first to shout 'yellow car' when you spot one gets a point.

Before I started this game, I thought yellow cars were rare. It was not something I'd ever noticed. Now I see yellow cars everywhere. It is not that the number of yellow cars has changed, but my brain has been conditioned to notice them.

When you actively seek to Notice something, you attune your senses and begin to consciously see more of that thing. You become more observant and may become more curious and knowledgeable about what you are noticing. I am sure you have observed this yourself. It happens when you are considering a major purchase; you might begin to observe other people's shoes, cars or porch designs. Things that otherwise would pass you by. You get curious, notice details and begin to think more clearly about what you want.

> *'When you don't notice consciously,*
> *you can miss important and critical issues.'*

When you don't notice, or don't pay attention, you miss things. It may just be that you miss a beautiful day or don't spot yellow cars. More importantly though, at work when you don't notice consciously, you can miss important and critical issues. Mistakes might happen or opportunities might pass you by.

The solution: Notice intentionally

It is estimated that humans are taking in up to 11 million pieces of information each second through all our different senses. This is a lot of information. The same report suggests you can only consciously process up to 50 pieces of information in your brain at any one moment in time.

That leaves 10,999,950 pieces of information that you are not noticing, which is processed subconsciously.[2] How do

---

[2] *Encyclopaedia Britannica*, 2021.

you decide which 50 to focus on at any one time? The answer is: you are most likely on autopilot and your subconscious has made that decision for you.

Imagine you are shining a torch in a dark room. As you scan the torch around the room you notice different things. If you only ever shone your torch in one direction, that is all that you would see. To notice the whole room, you would have to systematically shine your torch from one end to the other.

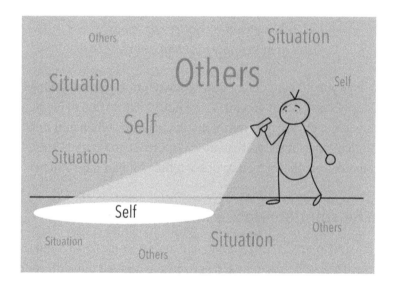

That is what I am asking you to do by Noticing intentionally: to be consciously aware, to focus actively, to be open to receiving different information into your conscious brain.

Neurologically, what you are doing is helping your brain rewire how it processes things. You are checking that your subconscious programme, your 'autopilot', is wired in the way you want it to be, rather than the way that has just happened throughout your life up to now.

You can intentionally choose to notice more in three core areas. Think SOS.[3]

Notice *Self*	Notice *Other(s)*	Notice *Situation*
What am I thinking? What am I feeling? What 'programmes' am I running: mindset, pre-judgements, bias, patterns etc.?	What are they saying? How are they saying it? What are their moods, attitudes, behaviours and patterns?	What's going on right now? How might the environment be shaping things? What about the bigger picture and the smaller detail?

By intentionally shifting our focus between these three areas, we build up a more complete picture of what is happening in the world. The more we notice, the more informed we become. The more informed we become, the more effective we will be.

So, let's drill a little deeper into how we can become more effective in our noticing.

---

[3] See the image and explanation of SOS, *Self*, *Other*, *Situation* in Chapter 2.

How do you become more effective at noticing?

Here are three ways for you to actively shine that torch on different areas of the darkened room. Three actions you can take to be more effective at noticing.

Action 1: Self – Notice what you are noticing.

As you notice things, it helps to Notice *what* you are noticing. Go with me on this.

I'd like you to look at the following three images. As you look at them for about a minute each, write down what you notice about each image. What do you notice for your*self*, the *other* or the *situation*?

Image 1	What I Notice

Image 2	What I Notice

Image 3	What I Notice

Remember the other 10,999,950 bits of information? Your brain is building pathways to process this information. Humans are sense-making machines. It is one of the things that makes us so successful – we spot patterns, trends, opportunities. Humans learn from experience and build brain pathways to be able to react quickly.

Much of the sense making you do is based not on fact, but on things you are holding on to as if they were fact – i.e. your emotions, your opinions and your internal beliefs.

How you interpret the information you take in depends on how you feel about it.

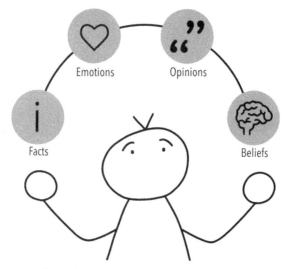

Figure 5 Juggling facts, emotions, opinions and beliefs

Take a look at what you have written down for each image. Against each thing you noticed, mark down if this is a fact, or if it is based on your feelings, your experiences or your opinions.

What did you notice? How much of what you noticed about each image was based on your emotions or beliefs? What can you state as fact about them?

Image 1 often elicits responses such as 'angry, patronizing, bored, fed up, my dad, Uncle Jim, my teacher, my old team-mate'. These are all your brain's interpretations, trying to make sense of what you see. When I mention this and then ask you to notice again for the *facts*, your response generally changes to a man in a white top, glasses, arms folded.

You have refocused, noticed what you are noticing.

Image 2 also may kick off some strong emotions. If you strongly identified with one of the teams, you may be strongly committed to which side has caused the infringement of the rules that the ref is currently carding. If you dislike football, in general, you may mention a lack of respect or shifting blame in the face of being caught out. But the picture is unclear as to which team is being carded, or who has caused the infringement. You interpret the image and the story behind it based on your opinions, beliefs and emotions about what you have noticed.

With Image 3, some people feel profoundly guilty, worried and anxious about the future, saddened by human behaviours. Others feel manipulated by an obviously faked image. Your interpretation here is probably based on your belief system. Do you believe this is true? Do you feel this is authentic? Do you trust what the image is trying to portray? Or do you resent it somehow?

Notice what you are noticing. Is it a fact or have you told yourself a story?

I was delivering an online workshop earlier this year. One of the attendees couldn't stop giggling. It made me cross because I believed they were having another conversation whilst pretending to be engaged in the course.

My colleague reminded me that this was the story I had created, not the facts. Indeed, when I asked the giggler, it turned out one of the images reminded him of a former boss and it had made him giggle; once he had started, he couldn't stop. The story I had told myself was based on my insecurity, not the facts.

Why is it important to notice what you are noticing?

Have you ever been in a meeting where two or more people are battling it out, each sure that they are representing the true facts, yet each with a very different interpretation of the same situation? The problem is that people often confuse opinions for facts.

Your brain works so quickly that it is difficult in the moment to recognize if what you are noticing is a fact, a feeling triggered by what's happening or an opinion/belief about this. These three aspects are clearly very different. It is by noticing this that you prime your brain to think differently; you shine the torch in a different area.

When you notice things about yourself, you become more self-aware. In the example above, I noticed I was cross. When I realized this was due to my insecurity, I became more self-aware.

Self-awareness is an awareness of your own emotional state (emotional intelligence) and the impact this is having, *and* an awareness of why this is so. Do you have deep-held beliefs or value systems that are coming into play? Is your previous experience colouring this perception? What subconscious biases might you be running or patterns of behaviour? Is the other person hitting your buttons (or triggers)?

Self-awareness is vital in effective leadership or teamwork for three reasons:

1. **Relationships:** in any relationship with another person, you take up around 50% of the space. If you are unaware of what you are doing with that space, it has a huge consequence for the relationship. You can ultimately only change yourself. You can't make other people change.
2. **Bias:** we are all working from a perception and a position that might be incorrect, or at least incompatible with the current situation.
3. **Action = Reaction:** any approach from you will pretty much dictate how the other person responds, depending on the existing relationship dynamics.

You can also use this in your conversations with people. You can be clear about what is fact (e.g. the man is looking over his glasses) and recognize that you may have very different opinions or feelings about the situation (e.g. he is judging me).

Action 1 summary

Notice *Self*: how you feel, what you are saying, what patterns or triggers you have, how you are phrasing things, what patterns you fall into with others.

Become more self-aware.

Action 2: Other(s) – Notice people, what they say <u>and</u> how they are saying it

It's not rocket science I know but it is very difficult to do well and consistently.

When you Notice someone, it shows you are paying attention to that person, that you care. We all want to be noticed. But what being noticed means is different for each person.

In work situations, you may notice that someone changes a habit. For example, they may begin to arrive late for work, not look right, over-react to a situation, or change the quality of their work.

You may notice that they are working really hard on some-thing, going the extra mile, picking up where others are drop-ping the ball, producing better-quality work or are super excited.

You also may notice that they are speaking less or with more confidence in a meeting. You may notice they are happy or sad or angry or passionate.

When you notice these details, it means you are giving that person the honour of attention.

1. It shows you value them. Being taken for granted is one of the worst feelings in the world and can set off all sorts of negative behaviours.
2. It demonstrates that you care, which is vital for gaining trust. Trust forms the basis of teamwork and collaboration. The better you know/trust people, the more likely you are to work on behalf of them and look after their interests.
3. You begin to actively seek and notice difference. Sometimes people feel uneasy expressing different opinions or ideas. However, if you want new solutions to old problems, you need to start looking at them in different ways. If you wish to create an atmosphere where people feel able to step up and speak out, you have to lead by example.
4. You begin to understand them better. The more you know, the more you understand and the more you are likely to be able to empathize. As Abraham Lincoln said: *'I don't really like that man very much, I must get to know him better.'*
5. Taken together, you can see how this can deepen your connection with others and can increase your influence with them.

So, how do you truly notice someone?

We are all hardwired to notice certain things more easily than others. We are more likely to notice things that have changed, things that are bizarre, funny or visually striking. We are also more likely to notice things regularly repeated or already primed in our memory.

Use this to your advantage. Notice what is different.

To notice what is different, you have to know what 'normal' for that person might be like. So, start to notice this. Then you can get curious about the significance of the small changes.

FBI agent Joe Navarro got curious about a small change when he saw the murder suspect's eyelids come down and stay down when questioned about an ice pick. He recognized the significance and knew he was on to something. Navarro explains in his book *What Every Body is Saying* that he had grown up as an immigrant in the USA and had to compensate for his lack of English in his early years by watching and interpreting the body language of those around him. The skills this taught him were later honed during his career in the FBI. Navarro knew this movement in the eyes was not normal for that person. The suspect later confessed to the crime.

When people communicate, they do it through their words (what they say) and their tone of voice and body language (how they say it). I will explore more about this in the chapter on listening but for now you need to know that noticing both what people are saying and how they are saying it is vital to effective communication. This doesn't mean that you need to become body language experts like Navarro but that we need to tune in and become curious about both areas.

Action 2 summary

Notice *Other(s)*: how they look, what words and phrases they use, what they are not saying, how they are saying things and what is different.

Become more aware of others.

Action 3: Situation – Zoom in and out to explore your situation

The situation has a major influence on how you behave. Noticing the context around you gives you situational awareness.

How do you notice the situation? Here are five questions to help you consider the situation:

1. What's in front of you? The immediate presenting issue.

    Whether you are facing a crisis, a performance issue, a general catch-up or brainstorming creative ideas, each of these will begin to dictate your approach.

2. What's behind you? The history or background.

   Have you been in a similar situation before? What does that experience suggest may happen? Is that helpful or not?

3. What's around you? The environmental context.

   Are you on a Zoom call, communicating by email, sat opposite each other in your office, on the beach or in a meeting room? Our environment affects our interactions.

4. What's above you? The bigger picture.

   What are the drivers here: corporate and individual? What impact is the team or organizational culture having? Are there systemic or political issues at play?

5. What's below you? Your certainty in the situation.

   The more complex or uncertain the issue, or the muddier the ground you are walking on, the less likely there is to be one definite answer.

You may well come up with more contextual areas to notice and I am sure that once you start noticing things, you will spot more.

As you get better at it and more practised, you will find you automatically pick up on some of these areas. Keep sweeping that torch around the room to notice more.

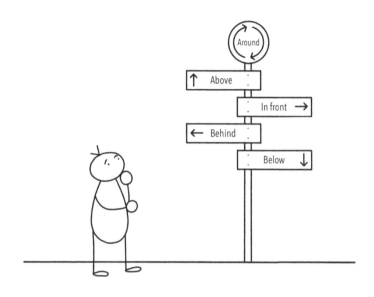

Action 3 summary

Notice the *Situation*: shift your viewpoint to look above, below, in front and behind you, notice what is the same and what is different.

Become more situationally aware.

An exercise in noticing

Let's explore all these areas in a short exercise. I'm going to use a story to show how the information you notice impacts your judgement of a situation. As you read this, imagine yourself as the person in this story and notice, as the story unfolds, how your judgement of the situation and people around you changes. You might like to stop every now and again to assess your judgements.

Make a note of your thoughts in the blanks before you read the next section.

You are on the London to Glasgow train. It's crowded as the earlier train was cancelled, and it is the slow train. You are sitting at a table, in the aisle seat, trying to get some work done. Your laptop has low battery.

Notice: What might be going on for you right now, given this situation?

You notice the other people around the table: the man sat opposite you looking at an iPad, the sleeping older woman next to you, the young man at the other seat apparently hardwired into his phone screen. Your laptop is low on battery, but the sleeping woman is in the way of the plug socket. There are four kids at the opposite seat table, with no obvious adult. It's noisy.

Notice: What judgements are you making about these people based on the small amount of information I have given you. Be honest with yourself.

You think about the long workday you have had. It largely feels pointless: Marketing haven't listened; sales are not happening; you have a new report to be done for 9am tomorrow morning; things are kicking off back on site; you need to be back there.

Notice: How does this affect your judgements? What are your thoughts and feelings? How does this impact on your perspective of the world?

The situation changes. The kids opposite start to kick off. They are running riot, squabbling, standing on the seats, going up and down the aisle, loudly watching videos. 'I'm hungry,' whines the smallest.

The older child approaches the quiet man opposite you. 'Dad, can we have money?' You notice he gives them some cash, without comment. He says nothing about their behaviour. They come back and load up with sugary snacks. The noise levels and behaviour get worse. He just sits there.

The train empties a little at Warrington. The kids start fighting. The father does nothing, carries on looking at his iPad.

Notice: What are your thoughts now? Judgements about the dad? What do you think of him? How are your views impacted by facts, emotions, opinions, beliefs; your views on good parenting? Is your opinion appropriate? How does it affect how you feel?

As the train reaches Lancaster, the kids are screaming, crying and there's an argument. Dad silently hands them his iPad. The older one plugs them into films. What a relief! It all goes quiet. You turn to the man. There is now just you and him at the table.

Notice: What do you (honestly) want to say to him?

This is what you do say: 'Are these your kids?' 'Yes.' 'They always like this?' 'Not always,' he sighs. 'We are on our way to family in Glasgow. We have just come from their gran's funeral... my mum.'

As he looks up, you see tears in his eyes. You see the grief etched into his face.

Notice: Now what might you think? What might you say to him? What do you want to do? How might that make you feel?

As you have read this story, what has changed for you? How did your emotions shift as the story unfolded?

What were the discomfort points for you?

What assumptions did you make – what stories did you create in your head about the characters as the story unfolded and how did this change?

Notice: What were your thoughts from doing this exercise?

Noticing what you find easy

You may have read this chapter and be thinking 'Holy Moly. Honestly, I have to start to notice all that??? It's too much I don't know where to start so I'll put it in the "too hard" box.' Maybe the following suggestions will help you get going.

Pick one of the areas (*Self, Other(s)* or *Situation*) and actively seek to notice something in it. You might decide in your video call to notice something about other people on the call. Or the effort they have made today. Or maybe that you are really looking forward to this meeting, or that you are facing something uncomfortable that you haven't done before.

You may like to keep a little diary. Make a note of what you have noticed that is different each day.

If you are not sure where to start, I usually recommend you kick off with the context. It is the element that is easiest to spot. Has your partner cleaned the house? Did someone hold the door open for you? Was your coffee cup moved from your desk and washed up? Is your colleague wearing a new jacket? Has the first snowdrop come out? Notice the positive things first.

By looking for these things, what else do you notice? And what else?

What this does is start to hone your antenna for noticing and to make you more connected to the environment around you. We are often so busy or disconnected as we walk through the world – answering texts, on the phone, speeding from one thing to another – that we don't stop and notice.

Try it.

What to watch out for

As you actively seek to Notice more, here are a few things to watch out for.

Focusing on the negative

We are naturally biased. We are predisposed to look for things that back up our existing worldview. When we get caught in a negative spiral, noticing more negatives is unhelpful.

Some days I feel like I do everything in the office. 'It's so unfair,' says my grumbly internal voice. I start to blame my colleagues for not pulling their weight. I start to notice how messy the office is, how much washing up is left in the kitchen, how the bathrooms are left in a mess. I notice more of the bad things because my focus is on the negative.

If I had questioned my mindset and actively looked to notice things that challenged what I was expecting to see, I might have noticed that I am often brought coffee, that the office is clean underneath the superficial mess, that I am often shielded from the administrative stuff, especially when I have been sitting at my desk until late in the night writing.

I know (because I teach this stuff) that when I focus on noticing the positives, I actively increase engagement, helpfulness and cooperation, if not collaboration. Just because I teach it though doesn't mean I am perfect. Not by a long way. We are all human. But it does make me more rueful when I realize what I am doing.

Seeing what you expect to see

> *'Whatever you hold in your mind will*
> *tend to occur in your life.' – Anon*

Once you believe something is true, you see the whole world through that lens. Your belief will look for evidence that proves it to be true and discount anything else. Nowhere is this more evident than in an early theory on motivation, McGregor's Theory X and Theory Y.[4]

Theory X managers believe that people are inherently lazy and need pressures or incentives to get them to work: they are the Stick and Carrot managers. Theory Y managers believe that people are inherently self-starters and can be trusted to manage their own workloads with minimal intervention from the manager. The problem is that both are self-fulfilling prophecies. How you manage people shapes how they respond, how they respond shapes how they behave, how they behave shapes what you notice and what you notice shapes how you choose to manage them.

So, the challenge to you is this: to what extent is what you are seeing because you expect to see it? Go to work and actively seek something that challenges your viewpoint of the world. It might be that you think your teammate is lazy. Or you think your boss doesn't care. It might be that you believe the company wants its pound of flesh from you and doesn't care about the impact.

What might the evidence be for the other way round? How might this change your thinking and help you to develop a more accurate picture or different viewpoint?

---

[4] Douglas McGregor, *The Human Side of Enterprise.*

Notice summary

- ✓ All you notice is not all that there is. Instead, what you notice is a mere fraction of what is going on in your world.
- ✓ Focusing your attention is like shining a torch in a dark room.
- ✓ Develop your ability to notice. Be more intentional in noticing what's going on in your world.
- ✓ Think SOS. What do I notice about my*self*? What do I notice about *others*? What do I notice about my *situation*?
  - ➤ Notice what you are noticing. Is it facts, feelings or opinions? – become more self-aware.
  - ➤ Notice people, what they are saying and how they are saying it – become more socially aware.
  - ➤ Change your viewpoint to notice what is going on in your world – become more situationally/ strategically aware.
- ✓ Be prepared to challenge your beliefs and assumptions and take small steps every day to pay attention to different things.

But noticing something only helps if you acknowledge what you have noticed. Which brings us on to the A of NALED.

Chapter 4
Acknowledge

Acknowledge: To accept, admit, or recognize something, or the existence of something, to show you have noticed or received something/someone, to publicly express thanks.

I remember being excited to start my new job in a larger organization, after many years of working in small businesses. One of the reasons I was excited was that we had a specialist marketing team to support my business development role and help to create the collateral I needed to do my job. I would get a much more creative and professional job, I thought.

As I started to work with them though, I realized that this wasn't going to be the bed of roses I had imagined.

Instead of being creative and making my life easier, all that seemed to matter was following a strict process and strict brand guidelines; bureaucracy ruled, and I felt the marketing team behaved like the brand police.

It was so frustrating! I would request marketing collateral, only to be told it was my job to write it and design it. I'd write it and design it, to be told it didn't fit the brand guidelines. They seemed to delight in making my life harder, not easier. There were numerous rows.

Our relationship got worse as I fought for great designs and great messages, while they fought for brand consistency. We could not agree.

When eventually I asked for help to get my point across, my boss refused. 'You need to work this through, Lucy, not me. Start from where we are, not where you think we should be.'

He helped me acknowledge the situation as it currently was: that branding was a big deal to them. If I acknowledged and began to understand their point of view, I could influence the future. Head-to-head we would get nowhere, but side by side we could progress.

I began to enter negotiations instead of battles with the marketing team. I acknowledged their position and so began to understand it. When I did this, they began to listen and value my position too. We improved our relationship and together took a step forward. Together, we created something better.

In the last chapter, I asked you to Notice more. Now I am asking you to Acknowledge what you have noticed. By doing this you make it real; you can begin to work with it. By acknowledging, you are not judging something to be good or bad; you do not have to have an opinion either way – it just is. You can't change what you don't acknowledge.

But if you have noticed something, then surely you are already acknowledging it?

Not necessarily. You need to acknowledge if the thing you have noticed is having an impact (spoiler, it probably is) on the current situation. This leads us to the main problem. When what we notice is difficult, we pretend not to know.

The problem: We pretend not to notice

How many of these scenarios have you found yourself in?

Self

You notice something wrong in your body, maybe a strange lump or a rising sense of stress, but you choose to ignore it. To pretend you haven't noticed.

Other(s)

You notice a growing sense of unhappiness in a colleague, or conflict between two team members, a worsening relationship with a key stakeholder or increasingly poor behaviour of a member of staff but you choose to overlook it and hope it resolves itself.

Situation

You notice that your business is struggling to keep up with changes in the world, but you choose to try and 'guts it out' by doing what has always brought you success in the past.

Or maybe you are choosing to disregard some of the really big stuff, like the effect that recent events had on people's mental health or the growing impact of climate change and the hard choices this presents to you.

Everyone is prone to ignore things, or pretend they don't know. When things are scary, unknown or threatening, you are more likely to fall into this trap. The trouble is that sticking your head in the sand rarely works: the issue you ignore just gets worse until you can ignore it no longer.

The solution: Acknowledge the good, the bad and the ugly

The good news is that acknowledging things is not just about facing up to the scary issues. Acknowledging is also about showing that you have noticed or received something and publicly expressing thanks.

When you **Acknowledge the good** with others, you show you care, you build trust, increase connections and develop your relationships. It can be used to explore diverse viewpoints and build deeper understanding to aid decision making. Acknowledging the good is extremely powerful.

Sadly, in environments where you are only as good as your last set of results, acknowledging the good is rarely done well or consistently.

Acknowledging the bad and the ugly takes courage, especially when you don't know the way forward.

In a team setting, acknowledging a tough situation is a core aspect of leadership. It is raising and seeking to address the elephant in the room without having all the answers.

> *'Acknowledging a tough situation is a*
> *core aspect of leadership.'*

'It doesn't make sense to employ smart people and tell them what to do; we hire smart people so they can tell us what to do,' said Steve Jobs.[5] Yet many leaders feel they must have the solution first. Great leadership is not about having all the answers; it is about having confidence in yourself and your team that you will find the way forward together.

As with noticing, it is important to be clear about whether you are acknowledging facts, feelings or opinions/beliefs. Acknowledging emotions can be particularly challenging and it's probably helpful to look at this first before I get into how you can acknowledge effectively.

Acknowledging emotions

Emotions colour everything.

In *Star Trek*, we were taught that Spock's lack of emotions makes him into a kind of supercomputer. But real life isn't like that. People unable to feel emotions can struggle to make decisions.

---

[5]   Steve Jobs, *Steve Jobs: His Own Words and Wisdom.*

In his 1995 book, neuroscientist Antonio Damasio describes the case study of his patient 'Elliott' whose life was turned around after a brain tumour wounded the frontal lobe tissue in his brain.[6] Elliott luckily survived with all his cognitive facilities intact, but he could no longer feel or recognize emotion. The impact was he could no longer make decisions. He struggled to interpret the world around him as there was just too much information to process but too little to aid him to make a decision either way.

Emotions are how you interpret the world. Acknowledging how much you are driven by them, judge by them and are hijacked by them is a major starting point in emotional and social intelligence.

For many traditional industry backgrounds, emotions have somehow been seen as fluffy and unhelpful. It seems much better to hide or even bury them. As a colleague drily remarked to me recently, 'Beware: when you bury emotions, you bury them alive.' Not acknowledging emotions is rarely helpful.

> *'Beware: when you bury emotions,*
> *you bury them alive.'*

---

[6] Antonio Damasio, *Descartes' Error.*

Emotions are incredibly powerful. Positive or negative, they are there whether you like it or not. You cannot ignore them, but you can reduce their power by acknowledging them.

In a workshop with a group of project managers, we were discussing the difference between facts, emotions and opinions.

'I hate people who bring emotions to work,' stated a senior project manager in construction (I'll call him Dave).

I asked him to expand.

'Well, those people who bring emotions into work... There is no place at work for emotions – it's just wrong. You should leave them at home.' (He was becoming increasingly agitated.) 'Why do people feel the need to bring emotions into what could be a logical technical discussion? Then they start talking about how they "feel" and all the decent conversation goes out the window. It's ridiculous and shouldn't be allowed...'

'What do you notice here?' I asked the group, 'Do you agree with Dave?'

'Well, it's ironic that Dave is talking about there being no place for emotions whilst displaying very strong emotions,' another group member replied.

Dave stopped saying what he was about to say and reflected, 'Oh. Yes. I suppose I am being really emotional there, aren't I?'

Fair play to him for realizing so quickly the paradox of the situation and having the personal wherewithal to admit that what he was saying and what he was displaying were completely at odds with each other. Do you know anyone like Dave?

How do you acknowledge?

Again, you can follow SOS – *Self, Other(s), Situation*. You have already seen the value in being systematic about Noticing across these three areas. Unsurprisingly then, you also need to Acknowledge what is going on in your*self*, with *others* and in your *situation*.

Acknowledging self

Acknowledging your emotions

As we saw in Dave's story, it is very easy to be completely unaware of your emotional state and, consequentially, the impact this is having on you, the people around you and on your situation. If you ask people how they are feeling, they will often struggle to come up with the right words and regularly resort to the standard reply, 'I'm fine!' 'Fine' can range from depressed to fuming, from OK to delighted. Many people are just not very good at both Noticing and Acknowledging their feelings.

One way around this problem is to rate how you are feeling on a scale of 1–10 from negative to positive. Try this now. On a scale of 1–10 how are you feeling right now? Notice and Acknowledge how you are feeling. It doesn't take long, does it?

And now a challenge. For the next week repeat this exercise at least four times during your day and jot down your scores in a little diary. You might want to set an alarm on your phone or computer to remind you.

In taking up this challenge, I believe you will notice two things. Firstly, you will become much better at noticing and acknowledging how you are feeling. Secondly, you will almost unconsciously find yourself doing things that make you feel more positive.

Research suggests that the area of the brain that regulates emotion is also the one that identifies it.[7] So, if you identify or name an emotion, you start the process of regulating it. We will explore this further in the 'Acknowledging others' section below.

Acknowledging the facts to yourself

Acknowledging things to yourself is often done silently, in your own head. When you notice something about yourself, you may well decide not to share it. Equally, when you notice something about others or the situation you are in, it is not always appropriate to acknowledge publicly what you have noticed.

Even if you choose not to share something, it is important to acknowledge key facts by making a mental note of what you have noticed. You may find it helpful to do this by writing something down. I find this particularly helpful in meetings. When I jot something down it allows me to acknowledge its importance and then to put it to one side. This allows me to notice and refocus on what others are saying rather than what I am feeling or want to say.

---

[7] For more information, see work by Torre and Lieberman on affect labelling, 2018.

Acknowledging your biases

Some years ago, my sister took me on a walk on the hills, saying she needed to tell me something. She looked very distracted. Very nervous. This was clearly important.

'Lucy, I have something I need to tell you,' she said. She then fell silent.

'Who is she?' I asked.

'How did you know?'

'I didn't, but you were so nervous, it had to be something big.'

We chatted away and she told me how she had found happiness with a woman. This was a completely new situation for me. At that stage of my life, my sister was the first person close to me that had chosen to come out to me personally. I had never been here before.

Mostly, I was just fine about it, but I noticed this little thing deep inside. A little voice that said, 'oh that's a shame'.

I could have ignored it, but I chose to acknowledge it was there and explore it. What bias was this? What pre-judgement was I making? I was pretty shocked at myself and ashamed that the little voice was there. So, I made sure I explored the thought further.

'That's a shame because my little sister will never be able to have kids like I have...'

Obviously, once I took it out and looked at it, I realized it was not true. That piece of cognitive bias existed in my head, and I had had no idea about it. It was only by consciously acknowledging the thought that I gave myself the ability to change it.

I am not proud of the realization that I am not as 'woke' as I thought I was. But until that moment I had no idea that that judgement existed inside my head. How could I? We can't prepare ourselves for all eventualities.

You may judge me for this story. I ask you not to. We are all works in progress. If I claimed I was perfect, you wouldn't believe me. And so it should be. Part of being human is to have deep-ingrained biases.

Diversity is all around us, whether in skin colour, body shape, body functionality, cultural norms, gender, sexuality, the way our minds work, our health, our likes and dislikes, our knowledge and experience, our education, our preconceived ideas... The list goes on.

Having diverse teams and workforces has been demon-strated time and time again to be better. But having diversity around us is challenging. Just as in my experience above.

The first step is to acknowledge that you are biased: we all are.[8] Once you have acknowledged this fact, the second step is to listen to that little voice in your head and acknowledge it, no matter how ugly it might be. Acknowledging an issue is the first step towards solving it.

*'Acknowledging an issue is
the first step towards solving it.'*

What are the deep-seated opinions or 'rules' that you have in your head? They often stem from how you were brought up, early experiences or the society/culture that you inhabit. Some of these biases and judgements may be helpful to you. Some of them not so much. Look them in the face and ask yourself if you want them to be there. It's not easy to do but it helps you learn.

Now that I have dealt with that little voice in my head, I no longer feel that way. It does not cloud my judgement and I am able to be truly happy for her.

---

[8] See Chapter 6 for a sample of some common cognitive biases in all humans. There are many more at play.

Acknowledging others

Acknowledging others verbally

The most open way of acknowledging others is to do it verbally. This can feel courageous at times as you make yourself a little vulnerable to the possible repercussions of publicly acknowledging a potential tough fact or issue. Here are some examples.

- I've noticed that your body language has changed as we've gone through this.
- I notice you are not coming to the coffee shop at lunchtime anymore.
- You seem disappointed.
- I recognize the level of research that went into that presentation.
- I notice you are behind your deadlines this week.
- I acknowledge you have a different viewpoint on this...
- I'm sensing my own emotional reaction to this situation.

To do this well, simply state what you've noticed, not what you might think about it or load it with emotion and judgement. This way, you allow the other person to open up further.

One way to do this is to reflect back to the person the emotions that you have noticed. Try using the following phrase: 'You seem *(insert the emotion you have noticed)* by this' and see what happens.

You might get the emotion wrong; that is OK. It can help to open up the conversation, help the other person express how they really feel and demonstrate that you care.

> I was demonstrating NALED in front of a group the other day, and my willing volunteer was telling me about the situation he found himself in. I acknowledged the emotions specifically.
>
> 'You seem upset by that,' I said.
>
> He countered me: 'I'm not upset; I am angry and feel slighted.'
>
> When we later discussed the conversation in the room, he told me that he had not realized how he felt until I got it wrong. It didn't matter that I had got it wrong; what mattered is that he then felt able to confront how he did feel.

Acknowledging others non-verbally

Non-verbal communication is a powerful way to acknowledge others, e.g. a hand on the shoulder, a nod of the head, a smile or a small act.

> I remember when I was younger being incredibly cross with my father. It was a significant issue and took me some time to get over. He is not someone that talks about emotions openly, despite clearly feeling things deeply.
>
> He knew I was cross and felt bad about what he'd done. I remember the day when I realized I had forgiven him, but I didn't know how to let him know. So rather than say anything, I brought him tea in his office, then stayed to chat and to help with tidying and filing. By these actions, he knew what I was trying to say. He smiled and accepted the actions and we moved on. For him, openly acknowledging his behaviour and my forgiveness would have been too hard. So, we did it differently. It worked.

One simple way to acknowledge someone's emotional state is by changing your body position or the pitch/tone of your voice to match theirs. For example, you can lower your voice and sit back to match someone who might be sad or up the tempo of your speech to match someone who is more excited or positive. You can mirror their movements – if they sit forward, you sit forward. This happens naturally when you are engaged in a conversation and can be used intentionally to acknowledge someone. Try playing with this. You will find that small changes in your tone and body language can often have a big effect.

Name it to tame it

You can take this one step further when you are in situations of high emotion or conflict. You can use Dan Siegel's method *Name it to tame it* described in his book *Whole-Brain Child*.[9] Siegel uses it with children, but it is effective with adults too. This is where you Acknowledge the emotion specifically by naming it, in order to turn down the level of emotion.

As previously mentioned, the area of the brain that regulates emotion is also the one that identifies it. So, if you identify or name an emotion, you can start the process of regulating it.

This technique is not only useful in regulating our own emotions but also in helping others to regulate theirs. Doctors are taught how to use this technique with patients to help them to deal with the strong emotions often encountered with health issues. This technique of acknowledging the emotion takes the sting out of it, helps people feel heard and enables them to work with you to find a solution.

---

[9] Dan Siegel, *The Whole-Brain Child.*

This worked for Philippa, who managed the contracts within a major project. She wanted advice as to how to deal with a dispute with a construction contractor. The contractor was not adhering to the terms and detail of the contract yet expected payment to be released. He was also trying to go over Philippa's head to get it signed off by her boss.

The relationship had deteriorated and they were at an impasse. Philippa was angry with his attempts to sideline her and frustrated that she could not get the required information out of him to release the payment. She knew the lack of payment could jeopardize the relationship between the two organizations, not just the two people.

Philippa tried the *Name it to tame it* technique.

'I'm sensing that you are frustrated with me for requiring this detail. I hear that you are anxious to get this payment through and willing to try different options to get around me.' She Noticed and Acknowledged his emotions. By doing so, he was able to admit that was indeed his situation.

Philippa continued: 'If you want to succeed, you have got to work with me. By going over my head, it makes me feel angry and non-compliant.' She went on to highlight the options available.

She took the power of the emotion out of the conversation by naming them. This created the space for them to solve the issue.

The *Name it to tame it* technique means they are now having better discussions, acknowledging the different standpoints of the two different companies and coming up with more creative solutions.

Acknowledging our situation

I was in a meeting recently with a group of safety-focused senior managers in the engineering industry. I looked around our virtual room. All of us were of a similar age, of white British origin and, I suspect, extroverted. I was the only woman (and brought in to observe and talk about relationships – not an easy gig!). The first half hour involved the usual political 'shouldering up' as the distribution of power was tested.

It would have been very easy for this room full of people to stroke one another's egos, talk about how good the safety record was and how much it has improved, and how many qualifications their team members had. The similarity of background could have easily created a comfort zone, where there was little challenge or dissent and everyone agreed how marvellous their decisions were.

It could have been a worthless use of eight people's time.

We had one courageous man, however, who acknowledged the unquestionable.

'But have we really got it right?' he asked. 'We might have low safety incidences and be hitting our KPIs, but how do we know that there is not something big in the pipeline, something we are missing, something people are not telling us because they don't feel they can? I'm concerned.'

He challenged whether they were really all that good on safety just because they had the right qualifications and hit their KPIs.

'Do we have the environment in which people feel able to challenge or admit to a mistake? Do we have teams who are good enough at relationships to winkle out what is really going on and where systemic failures may lie? Do we have leaders who are humble enough to admit their processes might not be working?'

By acknowledging a potential weakness in his own organization, he created the environment in which others could admit weakness.

> By actively seeking dissent and voicing it, he opened up the floor to challenge and people looked at their own organizations differently and began to notice more.

What happens in your organization? When you raise a big issue in a meeting, what usually happens?

Maybe you have lots of people clamouring to give their opinion, nobody really hearing the point just raised but waiting to say their piece instead? Maybe you get a few loud voices that are always there holding the floor? Or maybe you get the HIPPO effect (Highest Paid Person's Opinion)[10] where once a senior member of staff has given their opinion, everyone else agrees as it seems the safest thing to do.

Teams often get what are known as echo chambers or groupthink, where people feel unable to raise a different point of view. This is particularly likely to happen where there is a lack of diversity in the group.

You can avoid this through facilitated use of acknowledging one another's points first. Raise a simple rule of speaking, ACE (Acknowledge, Check, Expand):

---

[10] The term was first coined by Avinash Kaushik in his book *Web Analytics: An Hour a Day.*

1. Acknowledge what you heard the person say before responding (What I heard you say is...).
2. Check (Have I got that right?) – if not, let them explain and then acknowledge this.
3. Expand (I'd like to expand or build on that by saying...).

You may find that in the early stages this needs a facilitator, someone willing to stop people and make sure they adhere to the format. Once you have done it in a few meetings, you should find this happens more naturally. You may be surprised at the ideas and diverse thinking that starts to emerge from the simple application of ACE.

What to watch out for

For yourself:

Watch out for beating yourself up about things when you have acknowledged something you don't like or something you could have done better. What is done is done. By acknowledging it you have started the process of learning, doing it better next time. If you don't like what you notice and acknowledge in yourself, you give yourself the choice to begin to change it. Now that is a powerful gift to yourself, not a stick to beat yourself with.

With others:

Acknowledging emotions can demonstrate empathy with a person. This is mostly a good thing. However, it can encourage more emotions to come out. Here are two things to be aware of should this situation happen.

1. Taking on their emotion

Emotional outpourings are OK. Move to listen, but don't take on their emotion. We are programmed to feel what others are feeling. Some people are very good at dumping their emotions on you. Don't take them on. They are not yours.

> I remember as a new coach, supporting local business owners during the immediate aftermath of a major flood. Wow. Now that was emotional. Exhaustion, anger, grief, frustration, fear... So many major emotions, papered over with a thin veneer of stoicism and resilience. By the end of the first week, I was completely drained. I felt it with them. I took on their pain. But I didn't need to. It wasn't helpful for them.
>
> What was helpful was me being there, acknowledging the situation, listening to them, exploring the potential futures. So, I learned how to not take on their emotions, how to let it go at the end of the day, how to be there for them without getting involved. You don't need to enter other people's dramas to be able to help them through it.

2. Sympathy can encourage a drama

Not always, but sometimes people need space to find their own way through a problem and the best thing that you can do is step away from the conversation. I remember recognizing this in myself when I was failing to learn to ski. The sympathy from the instructor made it worse and gave me permission to feel sorry for myself. I was better off working through it on my own.

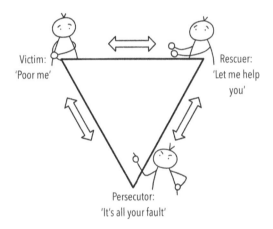

Figure 6 Developed from Stephen Karpman's Drama Triangle

At worst, you can become involved in what Stephen Karpman[11] described as a 'Drama Triangle'. Put simply, there are three mindset positions in this triangle: Victim, Persecutor and Rescuer. People that take on a Victim mindset are likely to suck you into the position of rescuing them

---

[11] See *A Game Free Life* by Stephen Karpman for more information.

from the person, or people, they believe that are persecuting them. This can become very dangerous and leave you locked into a position of continually having to support the individual who loves being rescued. If you make efforts to step away, you quickly become the new Persecutor.

> 'Do you know, Lucy, I find Acknowledge the hardest part to do,' said my coach colleague who I had asked to do a first draft read of this book.
>
> 'Listen is my stock in trade,' she said, 'Explore and Do are part of my coaching practice. I notice things – but do I always acknowledge them, especially to myself? Probably not. I wasn't expecting to learn anything from reading your draft version, but I have had a realization.'

Acknowledging is powerful.

Try it.

Acknowledge summary

✓ When you acknowledge what you have noticed, it demonstrates you have noticed, heard or appreciate something/someone.

✓ The act of acknowledging brings things onto the field of play; you accept, admit or recognize that it is what it is. You can't work with something unless you have acknowledged it.

> ➤ By acknowledging *others*, you demonstrate you care, which helps people feel valued and builds trust and engagement.
>
> ➤ By acknowledging *self*, what is going on for you, you give yourself an opportunity to do something differently, to rewire your automated responses and make better choices.

✓ Acknowledge the good, the bad and the ugly.

✓ In working with emotions try *Name it to tame it.*

✓ In challenging meetings, think ACE – Acknowledge, Check, Expand.

Chapter 5
Listen

Listen: *To make an effort to hear something.*
To pay attention, heed

Jan is a project manager on a nuclear construction site. Safety is paramount to all she does. One of her supervisors regularly fails the safety inspections on site. Jan usually brings him into the office and gives him a good talking to.

'After I've given him a rollocking, we usually don't really talk to one another for a couple of weeks, but then it is OK again,' she explained, 'then the issue happens again. It's just not working.'

Jan decided to try and approach the situation differently.

Instead of telling her supervisor off, she presented the report to him and asked him what he thought, and then she actively listened to him.

She heard about issues on site; she heard about staffing and resourcing problems. She heard how he didn't really understand why this inspection was important.

By listening, Jan began to truly understand, and her supervisor felt heard. The real issues came out and they found solutions together.

'We ended up with a very different outcome.' Jan told me. 'The relationship between us is loads better and I understand his issues and concerns more, and he understands mine.'

Now, instead of regularly failing the safety inspections, this supervisor runs one of the better-performing teams on site. Because she took the time to listen.

'Listening is a superpower.'

Listening is a superpower. It can unlock conflict, solve problems, inspire creativity, motivate, cut to the heart of things, empower and build trust. But like all skills, it takes practice.

Any old fool can be there whilst someone is talking; any old fool can give advice. But to actively listen? It is both a skill to give and an honour to receive.

When was the last time you properly listened to someone? Switched off your phone, zoned out from the distractions around you, turned off the voices in your head, stopped thinking about yourself and actually gave them your full attention?

For many people, it's not that often. If I am honest, I'm not always the best listener, especially for my family and friends... And I am a professional coach and facilitator: listening is my business.

Your listening skills are like any muscle or activity. If you are not used to using it, you are likely to be rubbish at it when you first start out *and* be very tired afterwards.

If you don't believe me, try it. Give someone your full attention for an hour. Listen to them and allow them to speak for the whole time. I'm not talking about a 'to-and-fro conversation,' I'm saying listen to *them*, hear *them*, ask *them* and follow where they want to go.

Now tell me afterwards: how do you feel? Exhausted? Wiped? Fulfilled?

Because here is the secret about active listening. It's not about you.

Let me say that again. Listening: It's. Not. About. You.

> *'Here is the secret about active listening. It's not about you.'*

The problem: Your listening is driven by your own agenda

Listening is on a spectrum that goes from ignoring someone to actively listening to them and truly understanding their position. It is easy to look like you are listening but not really be.

Stephen Covey summed it up perfectly: 'Most people do not listen with the intent to understand; they listen with the intent to reply.'[12]

You are predisposed to work off your own agenda. Your subconscious brain is continually scanning either for threats or things that will make you feel good. It is unsurprising therefore that in most of your conversations, your listening is driven by your own agenda. 'What are they saying that I like or dislike? What are they saying that may be a threat or an opportunity? What are they saying about the things that I want or need to know about?'

- As a manager, why would I want to listen to my team's ideas when I already know the best answers?
- Why would I want to hear their perspectives when I already know what is going on?
- Why would I want to listen to someone else's problems if that then leaves me feeling obliged to do something to help them out?
- Why would I want to ask them a question when I know that they will just drone on for ages? Frankly they are boring and don't interest me.
- Why should I listen to them when no one listens to me?
- Quite frankly, I'm too busy at the moment. Let's face it, listening to people is a 'nice to' not a 'need to'.

---

[12] If you do not know *The 7 Habits of Highly Effective People* by Stephen Covey, it is worth a read or listen.

I could go on. When listed like this it all looks pretty stark. I would be surprised if anyone would admit to thinking anything like this publicly: 'Sorry, I don't want to listen to you because I don't think that you have anything useful to say!'

When you are thinking these things, your thinking is driving your actions and you are not truly listening. You are probably pretending to listen though, as that's what humans do. The problem is that people pick up on this and can get pretty fed up with us pretty quickly.

The solution: Get off your agenda and give people a darn good listening to

The world is changing. In previous times, the preferred strategy to get more from people was to give them a 'darn good talking to', just like Jan in the story at the beginning. In a complex, fast-changing world where collaborative problem solving is often the key to competitive advantage, this approach is outdated. When dealing with issues of change, performance improvement, problem solving, and so on, you can't go far wrong by giving someone a darn good listening to. As Henry Ford said, 'With every pair of hands comes a free brain.' You unlock their brains by listening to people.

> *'You won't go far wrong by giving*
> *someone a darn good listening to'*

Effective listening, like any other area of performance, comes down to three things: capability (skill), capacity (time) and desire (will). Let's look at your will to listen first and what might motivate you to get off your agenda and give someone a darn good listening to.

Why should you listen?

Put simply, listening is at the heart of human connection and fulfilment, both at home and at work.

What would it be like to work in a place where you feel no one understands you, where you feel that you have no choice, and where you believe that people care more about the bottom line than you?

Maybe some or all of this is true for where you work. In work cultures where people only listen from their own agenda, this will be the inevitable result. If it is true in your workplace, it is bad news not only for wellbeing but also for the bottom line.

Humans fundamentally want to be understood, want to feel they have choice and want to feel cared for. Listening demonstrates care, builds understanding and empowers people.

> *'Listening demonstrates care, builds understanding and empowers people.'*

Listening demonstrates care

Listening encourages compassion and demonstrates care.

It is meaningful, builds trust and relationships, and encourages care and compassion amongst your team. To have a truly collaborative, high-performing team, trust, care and compassion for one another is essential.

Simon Sinek tells a great story about a group of riggers, who were being pulled in to be the crew for the biggest deep water drilling platform ever built, the Shell Ursa.[13] As such a massive and expensive operation, it brought with it all sorts of dangers and complexities. A properly tough job.

With safety the number one concern, the leader took his crew through an unusual team preparation; he got them together to talk about their emotions. The care and psychological safety that was built through understanding each other completely and acknowledging then listening to one another

---

[13] Simon Sinek, *The Infinite Game.*

created an awesome level of trust.[14] This trust, combined with their existing technical expertise, led to the best safety record and performance in the industry.

Listening empowers

By telling people what to do, you remove their ability to think for themselves. This either creates rebelliousness or adapted behaviours, where people only do what they are told. They no longer feel they even have a point of view, let alone feel empowered to share it, to act on it without being told. This can be actively dangerous, especially in the safety arena. By listening to what they think they should do, you'll unlock their brains, you'll engage and empower them in the solution. It might be different to yours, but that's OK.

Listening builds understanding

The act of listening to someone, to ourselves or to a situation gives us a deeper understanding of what is really going on. You listen to hear more, to discover more, to unearth more.

---

[14] Psychological safety is defined by Amy Edmondson in *The Fearless Organisation* as 'a shared belief held by members of a team that the team is safe for interpersonal risk taking.' It was found to be by far the most important dynamic of effective teams in Google's 2016 Project Aristotle research. See the bibliography for more details.

If you placed four people around the outside of a room and an enormous beachball in the middle, but only allowed them to see the ball from their angle, you might get quite different descriptions.

'It's pink'

'No, it's green.'

'I can only see yellow.'

It's only by combining all the viewpoints that you understand you are looking at a beachball.

Listening changes your thinking

By listening to someone, you learn. You learn about them for sure, but you often also learn about yourself – how much you want to butt in or advise, for example. Equally, you may well learn more about the context or situation in which you are operating. Listening to someone gives us the benefit of their perception or viewpoint. If you listen without bias, you can challenge your own thinking and see something from someone else's point of view.

How do you listen more effectively?

There are three core principles which underpin being a better listener.

1. Be fully present.
2. Ask simple, open questions.
3. Remain curious for longer.

Let's explore each of these now.

Principle 1: Be fully present

When was the last time you were telling your boss, partner or friend something important and they looked at their phone whilst you were talking? How did it make you feel? I demonstrate this in an exercise with groups, and even though people know it is a set-up, they still have incredibly strong reactions. The room will go from a buzz of conversation and interest to silence within about ten seconds.

And yet how many times do you do that to others? How many times do you look at your phone, check the time, do something else when others are speaking with you?

When you do this, you are sending a message that they are less important than whoever might just have caused your phone to buzz or your computer to ping. This is why the first principle of effective listening is to be fully present. Park the distractions, turn the phone or computer off; even letting them buzz on silent is a distraction to effective listening.

A good question to ask yourself to check if you are fully present is: 'Am I listening or am I just waiting to speak?' When I am waiting to reply, I am thinking more about what I am going to say next, or the brilliant question I am going to ask, or my take on what is going on, rather than actually listening.

If you find you are waiting to speak, jot down your thoughts on to a bit of paper and put it to one side, then continue listening. That way it's still there and you can judge if it is still relevant later.

If I have the intention to listen in order to understand, I begin to listen more actively and am more interested in what is being said. This means bringing my whole self to the conversation – listening with my whole body.

When you are truly listening to someone, hearing what is both said and unsaid, your whole body shows it. You are likely to be looking at the person, nodding and smiling, leaning towards them, matching them in pitch, pace and body language. Try deliberately using these as you learn to listen more, to show you are fully present.

When you are fully present to listen, you are more likely to hear both what is said and what is unsaid.

Listen to the words (what they said), listen to the music (the pitch and tone and emphasis in how they said it) and listen to the dance (their body language as they are talking to you).

Listen to the words

Language is an amazing tool to communicate with but it also shapes our world. The language you use tells much to the listener.

For example, if I tell someone 'You are an idiot,' it is very different to if I say: 'You are behaving like an idiot.' It is subtle but it is profound. The first speaks to the very person that they are. The second simply talks about their behaviour in that moment.

When I am coaching, I will often pay attention to certain words and phrases that people say. It tells me about little patterns or inner thoughts and judgements that people have made.

One of my clients used the words 'I should...' all the way through a session exploring her leadership of her team. When I reflected this back to her, it prompted a conversation about her belief about what a leader 'should do'. Who said what she should do as a leader? What would it give her if she did these things? How was she measuring her effectiveness as a leader and was it against the right things?

When she realized that the image of 'the perfect leader' that she had created herself was both unrealistic and probably quite inhumane, she let go of all the 'shoulds' and started to trust her instincts more. This changed her approach to leadership and shaped her team to perform way beyond expectations. This led her to develop a position of considerable influence within her organization.

Listen to the 'music'

The meaning of the words you say is changed by the sound of how you say it: the 'music'. This might be the tone of voice, how you pitch and emphasize the words in a phrase, the subtle sighs or stops.

Let me show you. Read the phrase below to yourself, placing the emphasis on a different word each time and see how it changes the meaning of the sentence:

'I didn't say he stole that money.'

Every single word in that sentence, if emphasized ahead of the others, changes the meaning of the sentence completely. If I emphasize the 'I', it suggests someone else said it. If I emphasize the 'didn't' it suggests my surety about what I did/ did not do. If I emphasize the 'say', it suggests I thought it, or I emailed it. If I emphasize the 'he', it suggests I said someone else stole it... And so on.

Often people raise the pitch of their voice at the end of a sentence to denote a question, or if they are unsure of themselves.

When you begin to actively Listen to the music, you can start to understand more about what is being said. You will Notice more and can Acknowledge what you have heard (weaving back in the strands of the NALED framework).

You already do this when you are talking on the phone; you will be listening harder to the subtle clues in the 'music' because you can't see the 'dance.'

Listen to the 'dance'

The 'dance' is the body language. The way people hold themselves, where they are looking, the facial expressions, and so on. Your body language is rich in expression and understood the world over.

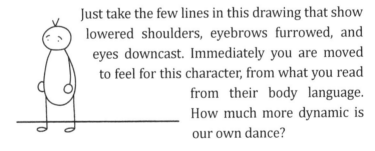 Just take the few lines in this drawing that show lowered shoulders, eyebrows furrowed, and eyes downcast. Immediately you are moved to feel for this character, from what you read from their body language. How much more dynamic is our own dance?

The dance is harder when you are on video calls. But it is still there. I have become more demonstrative when I am online these days in my facial expressions to communicate more effectively. Others do the opposite.

There is nothing wrong with pointing out someone's body language when it feels appropriate to acknowledge it. I might say – 'I notice you appear to be thinking hard about this.' Or 'I see a little smile on your face – tell me about that.'

You may not notice these things consciously but trust your instincts. As mentioned before, you are subconsciously processing millions of things every second. Tiny changes in expression and body language often have significant meaning.

Principle 2: Ask simple open questions

An open question is one that invites a variety of answers and allows someone to speak their mind and allows you to shut up and listen. A closed question only requires a yes/no response and then you have to ask another. It sends the other person down a specific route. An open question opens someone up; a closed one narrows them down.

Classic open questions start with one of the following:

Who, What, Where, When, How.

To remember these simply, think 'four bums on a bench (WWWWH).'

I recommend you try to avoid the 'why' question. The 'why' start to a question is often loaded with emotion. People don't hear, 'Why did you do that?' but, 'Why *on earth* did you do that?'!!

Figure 7 'Four bums on a bench'. Open questions: Who, What, Where, When, How?

A common trap is to start with an open question, then close it right down before you've finished.

> *How did you come up with that idea? Did you think it was the cheapest option?*

You can see here that the first question opens up thinking, whereas the second is closing or leading the thinking. Stop, shut yourself up. Leave it open…!

Another common problem is that the questions that people ask are far too complicated. You end up thinking more about your question than listening to the other person. My advice to you is to keep your questions as simple and as short as possible. Favourites of mine include:

> *Tell me about…*
> *Tell me more…*
> *I'm curious about…*
> *I'm wondering about…*
> *What else…*
> *Anything else…*

The underlying element here is not to anticipate what is coming next. It is easy to pre-judge and think you already know the answer. This is the same if you are listening to another person, listening to your inner voice or listening to the wider voices and trends in the environment around you. Switch off that judgement, ask open questions, then sit back and truly listen. You might just learn something.

Principle 3: Remain curious for longer

Being curious is the start point for learning, for understanding. Having an attitude of curiosity helps to switch off your judgement and sense-making machinery and keep your pathways open. It helps you remain open to different options, to learn and to discover new opportunities.

Keep them thinking

Keeping the other person doing the thinking has two main advantages. Firstly, it empowers them to solve their own problems by actively demonstrating you believe they can. Secondly, it means you don't have to do the  thinking for them – it makes your lives easier. When you have a tough job already, why make it harder?

I have a mental image of the thought bubble that I am attempting to keep over their head not over mine. There is a classic acronym in coaching, WAIT – Why Am I Talking? Notice who is doing most of the talking here and who is doing the listening.

Keep your advice monster in check

What makes you the guru that knows all the answers? There is almost always more than one answer to a problem. And most of us are rebels at heart. You don't really want to be told what to do: you like to think you have done it all by yourself (and it's loads more powerful when you have).

Michael Bungay-Stanier introduces us to these little monsters in his book *The Advice Trap*.[15] People are hardwired to find answers. He talks about 'advice monsters' sitting on everyone's shoulders that just love to help people, fix problems or control the situation. These advice monsters leap in and offer advice to people before you have found out what the real issue is.

The problems with this are you often end up solving the wrong problem and, possibly even worse than that, you imply the other person is not good enough to solve the problem for themselves. Remember the story of me trying to fix my partner at the start of the book?

---

[15] Michael Bungay Stanier, *The Advice Trap*.

Slow down – use silence

Whilst it feels hard to give someone time to think about their answers when you already 'know' what the answer is going to be (and you are probably really busy), it is very powerful. Silence is one of the most powerful tools in your listening toolbox. Use it wisely. Use it regularly. Slow down and let them think. People like to fill silence!

Actively listening to someone opens them up. It allows them the chance to air their thoughts about a subject without risk of judgement. Many people find that just the act of talking something through helps them to reorder their thinking, or to identify gaps and priorities. Even if you say nothing at all, the other person will often solve their own problem.

I have one client who, every now and again, asks me to mute myself during our phone coaching conversations. This is so that she has no distraction from her thoughts whilst she is talking. No breathing, inadvertent 'mm-hmms' from me or hearing my pencil writing my notes.

I might as well not be there – I could get on with something else and just let her talk. But I don't. And she knows that I am listening hard. She doesn't want my opinion, my responses, my questions even. It is enough to know she is heard.

How do you know if the silence is too long? If you are not sure, ask: *'Do you need more time to think about that?'*

Creating the space for people to talk is also important in a group setting. In many tough jobs, it becomes the norm to hear the loudest voice in the room.

I was working with a group of construction managers, and the leader mentioned one girl in the team who he noticed was really bright, really capable but not very confident. 'I don't understand why she doesn't come forward more...' he said.

'Have you been in your meetings?' I asked, knowing the team of mostly older, male, extroverted, super-busy, stressed project managers don't necessarily allow for the less confident, more introverted thinkers to come forward. 'Fair point...' he smiled ruefully.

Some people need time to think things through; others think whilst they speak. Often our organizations are set up for extroverted thinkers. Give someone the silence they need to think it through. If you are noticing them, you'll know if they are still thinking.

Check to ensure you really understand

This means not jumping to conclusions straight away. Don't presume that you have understood. Keep checking whether what you are understanding is indeed what is being said.

Repeating back what you have heard is a really good way of both checking your understanding and demonstrating that you are listening. It also helps the other person to reflect and remember what they have said. *'What I've heard is...'*

Hopefully, you will have found something in the three principles, 'Be fully present', 'Ask simple open questions' and 'Remain curious for longer', that will help you to enhance your listening skills. Before we move on, I thought that it would be helpful to touch on how you can listen to yourself.

Listening to yourself

When I reflect on things to support my development, I might notice the thoughts that are going through my head, making sure I am aware they are just that, thoughts not facts. I might also listen to the words and language that I use, or the way I phrase certain things. I also listen to my instincts. I know I am sensing something – how do I listen harder to that? Where in the body am I feeling it? How do I allow my emotions to come and go?

A useful technique when listening to yourself that you might like to try is freewriting.

Take an empty piece of paper and a pen. Set a stopwatch for a maximum of six minutes.[16] Set your topic or question you want to explore, for example, 'I am feeling stressed because...' and just write. Don't think about what you are writing, just do it. You might be surprised at what comes out.

Bringing it all together

Whilst it is unlikely to follow this exact format, the framework below pulls together some great listening techniques and may give you a broad route map to follow in in your conversations with people.

Opening question – 'Tell me...'

Tell me suggests you want to know. It is not judgemental.

If you have noticed something in advance of your conversation, you might acknowledge this in your opening question, for example, 'I notice you appear uncertain about our new idea. Tell me your thinking on this.' Notice, Acknowledge and Listen in a nutshell. Boom!

---

[16] Six minutes is just enough. You will probably find your hand is starting to hurt at this point. Five minutes is not quite long enough... By keeping the time short, it focuses your mind and becomes something doable. This technique is from Gillie Bolton in her book *Reflective Practice*.

Dig a little deeper

Ask 'What is the REAL challenge here for you?' The presenting issue is often not the real issue.

'And what else?' or 'Anything else?' or 'Tell me more' are also good questions here.[17]

Use silence

If you are not sure what to say, don't say anything.

Give it back to them. Keep them thinking

'What should I do?' is a common question. Rather than respond with ideas and rush to solve the issue, give it back to them. 'Tell me what your thoughts are so far' or 'What is your best guess at the moment?'

Reflect back what you have heard

When you repeat back or summarise what you have heard, it lets someone know you have heard them, and can prompt additional thinking.

'So, what I am hearing is...'

---

[17] Adapted from Michael Bungay-Stanier's book *The Advice Trap*.

Constantly Notice, Acknowledge, Listen

Notice what is going on in yourself, with the other person and in your situation. Acknowledge what is going on (whether verbally or non-verbally) and go back to listening. This is an iterative process: keep going round the loop.

Finally, practise. You will get better at it and it will feel less clunky. The first time you do something new it always feels a little weird. That is OK. Keep going. Remember when you first started driving? Putting together all the different actions in order to set off (mirror, clutch, gear, mirror, over shoulder, accelerate, clutch, brake release... or something). You kangarooed, stalled – it felt clunky. Do you think about how to do it now or just do it automatically? It becomes the same with listening; if you persist, these behaviours will become second nature.

Something that might help you in your learning is to jot down some notes after a conversation to reflect on what went well or less well. I have included a table below that might help you in this. It takes discipline to do this consistently. I really struggled to keep a reflective log when I was seeking to improve my listening skills as part of a qualification in Executive Coaching. When I did, it really helped me to spot patterns and remember what worked with different people. Give it a try.

Listening reflections

What happened when I listened?	How well did I listen?	What was the most effective thing I did?	What could I have done differently?

Listen summary

- ✓ If you only do one thing from this book, take the time and give someone the honour of listening to them properly.
- ✓ Listening is a superpower that anyone can learn, but it needs practice, even if you only do it for five to ten minutes at a time. Start small.
- ✓ Give people your full attention.
  - ➤ Show that you are listening.
  - ➤ Listen to the words, music and dance.
- ✓ Ask simple, open questions.
  - ➤ Think 'four bums on a bench' WWWWH.
  - ➤ Tell me…? Anything else? I'm curious…? I'm wondering…?
- ✓ Remain curious for longer.
  - ➤ Keep them thinking.
  - ➤ Keep your advice monster in check.
  - ➤ Use silence.
  - ➤ Check understanding.
- ✓ Practise and reflect to keep getting better.

Chapter 5½

STOP and practise

*'Practice doesn't make perfect, practice
makes better.'*
My daughter, aged 8

Stop, take a minute or two and get this first bit right.

The natural break

There is a natural break between NAL and ED.

NAL is all about spending longer, opening your eyes, ears and self to learn more. It is the slowing down, the silence, the gift of time. Whereas ED is all about moving forward; finding solutions and making decisions.

People often rush to the ED. So, let's actively stop now.

I invite you to put the book down and practise Notice, Acknowledge and Listen. Give someone a darn good listening to!

Find someone you are comfortable to try this with. I suggest that you let them know that you are trying out a tool or model or process, so that you can get their feedback on it. If there are two of you both working on NALED, even better.

Set aside ten minutes, possibly fifteen if you need to catch up with them first!

I want you to truly Notice, Acknowledge and Listen to them.

Start by asking them a non-standard question. Perhaps one of the following.

'Tell me about a mistake you have made at work.'

'How has this last week been for you?'

'Tell me about your hopes or fears for the next few months?'

Your job is to NOT get drawn into a standard conversation.

Be curious, ask questions, keep it focused on the other person.	What do you notice – *Self, Other, Situation?*
Acknowledge what you have noticed.	Listen actively (stay quiet!).

After you've been talking intensely for ten minutes or so, draw it to a close and ask how the other person felt. What did they notice about the process?

If you can't find someone to practise with, try it in a live conversation. Be brave. See what happens and how it is different from your normal approach to a conversation.

'I liked the 1:1 coaching exercise – I learnt more from my colleague in 20 minutes than I did in three years of knowing them through work, as we had a much more meaningful conversation. I have definitely used this to get to know people more and to find out their

point of view and their drivers, which has been very
helpful at work and outside. Before I would be more
cautious of talking beyond social niceties.'

Yes, it will feel clunky at first. Doing something different
always does. But as my wise daughter said: 'Practice doesn't
make perfect, practice makes better.'

What to watch out for

Listening is tough. Especially if you start to do it more regularly. I try not to have more than four one-hour coaching
sessions in a day; three is better. It's hard work. So don't be
surprised if you are a bit mentally frazzled from listening
more.

Please do consider your personal mental wellbeing. Be kind.
Get outside. Do exercise. Eat well. It makes a big difference.

It would be wrong of me not to mention mental health, as you
may find that as you Notice, Acknowledge and Listen to people and yourself more deeply, you encounter concerns about
your own and others' health.

If you are concerned about someone, don't try and fix them.
Be kind. Listen, and if it is appropriate, encourage them to
seek professional help.

If you are concerned about yourself, it's much the same. Be
kind. Find people who will listen and don't feel judged if you

seek professional help (there is more information at the end of the book).

The main thing is if someone is wanting to talk about something deeply personal, you may never get beyond Listen. That is OK. You don't have to get any further. It is unlikely you will do any damage or hurt anyone further by giving them a darn good listening to. And it might just help.

How do I know?

Remember the story at the beginning with my husband? The more I suggested things to do, the more isolated and angrier he felt. Once I noticed this, I had to shut up, acknowledge that he felt the way he did and listen to him. That is really where I truly learned how to NAL. I would just shut up and let him talk.

It helped him through the worst bit. It strengthened our relationship. It gave me a new life skill. It gave me an appreciation of the gift of space and silence.

Eventually, some time later, he was ready to move to the E, to Explore. Are you?

Chapter 6
Explore

Explore: *To investigate systematically, examine; to search or seek; to discover, to travel*

'I've always got a queue at my desk,' said Mo, 'I don't have time to do all this talking stuff. I just need to crack on.' Mo was explaining to me how he was employed as a problem solver, to deal with the queue of lads at his desk (and it was mostly lads) wanting answers.

'I just have to get through the list of questions fast enough and solve the issues straight away,' he told me, 'I don't have the time to notice or listen or anything.'

The impact of Mo solving everyone's problems for them was, of course, that people constantly come to him to solve their problems. It was a self-fulfilling prophecy. The price of successful problem solving is more problems to solve. The other impact was that Mo became the 'font of all knowledge' and a potential pinch point in an organization – if he fell over (which, given the level of stress he was under on a daily basis, was quite possible), the company would be in trouble. Finally, he was no longer on the ground, walking the floor, able to turn his considerable expertise to the real problems.

By not stopping to listen, to find out what the real issue was and to notice what else might be going on, Mo became the risk himself.

In this particular instance, Mo bit the bullet, carved out time in his diary, spent a little longer with people and empowered them to find their own solutions. Before long, the problems coming to him changed, and he ended up uncovering a deep-seated but simple underlying issue that had caused months of problems. It was easily solved once he knew what it was.

Taking the time to Explore saved him a huge amount of time down the line.

'Taking the time to Explore saved him a huge amount of time down the line.'

How quickly do you leap into solution mode when someone comes to you with a problem? I know many people that rush in every time. It is really frustrating! What I want them to do is to Listen to hear the full problem so that we can Explore options together, but they leap into solution mode straight away. 'I was only trying to help,' they say.

The problem: You jump into solutions mode

In a busy, frenetic world it's very easy to jump into solutions mode. The old mantra 'if you want something done, ask a busy person' is true. You quickly solve things for people, tell them what to do, run a quick fix...

You might moan about constant demands on your time, and the ever-increasing size of your email inbox, but how much of this is a problem of your own making? Most people, especially those in tough jobs, love to jump into solutions mode.

If you are being truly honest with yourself, there is probably something you really like about this. It's good to feel needed, the superhero solver of problems. It's good to tick things off the problem to-do list; it gives you a sense of achievement. It feels good to be the expert, to have the answers, and sometimes that is a necessity. But be aware of the choice you are making.

Like any type of short-term 'fix', jumping into solutions mode has its downsides. In the rush to solve problems, fix things, rescue people, you can miss the nuance, miss bringing people with you and actively make the problem worse, just as I did in the opening story.

Being the 'problem solver' can create a vicious circle; whilst it fixes the short-term issue, it gives you a longer-term problem. Let me explain why:

Firstly:

The more that you tell people the answer, the more that people look to you for the answers. You become the 'Answer Dispenser'. Your workload will increase, and your stress levels will rise.

Thirdly:

The more you tell people what to do, the more you undermine their confidence and their long-term ability to solve their own issues. When people are excluded from the process of exploration, they can feel demotivated, ignored, side-lined, worthless and negative.

Secondly:

The more quickly you leap to solutions, the more likely you are to miss things. Yours is only one perspective of the problem; your solutions are drawn from one person's experience. You may address the symptoms of a problem but never get to the underlying cause.

How many times have you been sat in a meeting, thinking 'if only I'd been involved in this from the start, we'd have come to a much better/faster/more practical solution'? Did someone else giving you a solution to your problem make you feel better or worse?

John told me his story: 'I was brought into this company to be creative and part of an innovative, forward-thinking team. I re-homed my family for this role. However, instead of a creative role, I was put on the "pipes" and told what to do for four years. I don't see the point anymore.'

John became an actively negative influence in the organization as his experience had redefined him. It was sad and John decided to leave the company. If he had had the opportunity to explore, to challenge, to innovate, he could have been an asset. His disempowerment became an actively negative influence.

The solution: Slow down and develop a systematic approach to problem solving

There are times when all that is needed is to be with the problem, to Notice, to Acknowledge, to Listen. There are times though when you need to move to a solution, to Explore and to Do.

The Explore strand to weave into your conversations is to actively go and seek different options; to discover new ideas, opportunities, ways forward, options, direction or focus. Exploring is a curiosity thread to weave in when people begin to search for alternatives, for answers, or to uncover more.

Once you have truly listened to someone you can begin to explore 'what next?'. Exploration is a journey, an adventure. It can be fun, challenging but hard work. It can be playful or interrogative; it can be creative or systemic.

You don't have to have an explicit goal to explore, although often you reach Explore when you are seeking a way forward. It can help to have an idea of where you want to get to but be prepared to discover something new.

Why should you explore?

For self

When you don't explore things, you get stuck in a rut. You practise the same reactions over and over again until they are set in stone. You probably believe you are right and seek the company of people that agree, creating echo chambers where you reinforce one another's opinions and do not countenance challenge.

To explore *Self* is to find a way forward, to address the nagging doubt, challenge the unhelpful pattern or face the problems you have been putting off.

With others

When you don't explore things with them, people feel as if they are 'told' what to do and just want to stay being told what to do because it is easier. Humans are inherently lazy; they often take the easy route, the comfort zone. But this is demotivating, uninspiring, and leads to complacency.

To explore with *Others* is to help them to dig deeper, to discover new options and empower them to find their own way forward.

> As one line manager recently shared with me: 'By exploring the options with my supervisor, rather than telling him what to do, he came up with his own idea of how to solve the issue. Now he keeps coming up with more ideas to improve the project. It's great!'

Our situation

When you don't explore things as a group or organization, you get left behind and you miss things. As the world changes around you, you miss opportunities, trends and patterns. You'll create gaps in your knowledge and are more likely to make poor decisions.

To explore the *Situation* is to take a step back, take a more systematic look at the issues that you face and investigate what is going on in your world, discover diverse options and innovative ways forward.

How to explore

Exploring benefits from a considered and systematic approach. Our desire for quick answers often backfires when we realize the problem wasn't exactly what we first thought, or we hadn't fully considered the ramifications of potential solutions. I suggest you firstly explore the problem fully before you explore the solutions.

*'Explore the problem fully
before you explore the solutions.'*

I remember a coaching session with a senior leader in the nuclear industry. She wanted to find a way forward about a challenge she was facing and started racing into the potential solutions. Before she did though, I challenged her to spend time looking at the problem in more detail.

As we looked at it from lots of different angles and unpicked assumptions, politics and nuance, she realized that the potential solutions she had come up with were too much, too soon. She quickly moved to improve her knowledge of the problem. We didn't get to exploring solutions that day.

To fully explore, it helps to recognize your personal lens of knowledge, experience, emotions and beliefs.[18] This will

---

[18]   See Chapter 3 for more detail.

blinker your view. You are also hardwired to try and confirm your existing point of view. This is called 'confirmation bias'.[19]

In human relationships, complex projects and challenging problems, there is rarely a single 'right' course of action. Exploring in the context of NALED is actively seeking to challenge what you thought you knew.

You will be favouring information that confirms what you already believe or would like to believe. It happens all the time on social media, where the supporting algorithms actively promote views and opinions similar to yours. Be aware of this as you explore. Notice it. Exploring teaches you as much about yourself as about the issue you are unwrapping.

You can use explore to both zone in on a topic and to zoom out. Think about exploring like the shape of a capital T.

You explore across the topic or situation, as if it were the top line of a capital T. This helps you stay zoomed out and to discover different perspectives, different angles, different strategies. You then zone in and explore down the vertical bar to dig deeper

---

[19] See 'Examples of common cognitive bias' later in this chapter.

on one angle or element. What does this show up? Then, you can go back to the top bar again and find another perspective and dig deeper again.

You can apply this capital T idea as you explore first the problem and then the solutions. Just remember to keep using NAL all the way through this systematic thinking so you can pick up on nuance and use the process to best effect.

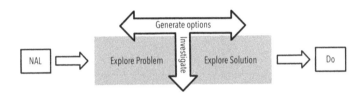

Exploring the problem

Exploring a problem has three key stages:

1. Defining the problem.
2. Analysing the problem.
3. Prioritizing the issues.

When you are exploring a problem or a challenge to understand it more and to actively challenge confirmation bias, it helps to look at it through a variety of different lenses. It is these lenses that will help you identify more about the subject.

Below is a simple problem definition worksheet. This framework of questions not only lays out what you believe the problem to be, but also the context within which it sits, and the boundaries for potential solutions. You can tweak the language to meet your needs.

The problem is:	Strategic context
What is the basic question to be resolved?	What is the bigger picture?
Present position	**Desired position**
Where am I now and what do I face?	Where do I want to be and what benefits will this bring?
Knowledge	**Assumptions**
What questions do I need answers for?	What assumptions have I made?
End user/Customer needs	**Wider relationships**
What does the end user or customer really want?	Who are the wider people involved in the problem and what power/influence/needs do they have?
Resources	**Constraints**
What resources do I have to play with? e.g. financial, people, relationships, things, ideas...	What are the constraints on me? e.g. time, money, support required

Defining the problem sets the context for exploring. You will often find when you start to dig a little deeper that the real issue might be sitting below the surface. There are a number of tools that you can use to analyse the problem. Two favourites of mine are the Fishbone Diagram and the 5-Whys.

When using a Fishbone Diagram,[20] you write the problem as you have defined it in the head of the fish and then populate the bones of the fish with the possible contributing causes to the problem. Some people like to use some generic headings to help in this, e.g. How might people, processes, resources or equipment be contributing to this issue?

The 5-Whys uses a similar but slightly simpler approach to dig deeper into the problem.[21] I know I said earlier that you

---

[20] Also known as the Ishekawa Diagram.
[21] Developed by Sakichi Toyoda, founder of Toyota, in the 1920s and used as a part of the Toyota Production System, later incorporated into the Lean methodologies.

shouldn't use the 'Why' question, but every rule should have an exception! When used in this very specific context it can add great value. Simply start with your problem and ask why you are experiencing this. Continue applying this process until you get to what you consider to be the root cause. Here is an example of this in practice for a problem I often experience when running online training programmes.

The problem: People don't engage as well in online workshops. This could be due to boring presentations, but I think I have done a good job of being engaging. So why else could it be?

> Why? Because they can more easily be distracted by other things.

> Why? Because they have emails, phones, colleagues, etc., easily accessible.

> Why? Because they are sitting at their usual desks using the same equipment they work on.

> Why? Because they can't easily find alternative options.

> Why? Because office designs were not set up for the way they are now being used.

By using either of these approaches to analysing the problem, you will often find that the defined issue is more of a symptom of some deeper underlying problem. The more you know, the more you will realize what you don't know. As you explore, sometimes the problem or options can get bigger. This is normal and a part of Explore. You need to push through the discomfort that this brings, knowing that you will eventually close things down again as you move into solutions and the Do of NALED.

> *'As you explore, sometimes the problem*
> *or options can get bigger.'*

The final stage of 'Exploring the problem' is prioritizing the issues. Whichever approach you may have used, the first parts of exploration are likely to have thrown up multiple underlying issues. The task now is to prioritize which issues to take forward as your focus for exploring solutions. Two questions will help you in this task:

1. Which of these issues, if we were to find a way forward, would have the biggest **impact** in solving the problem?
2. How much **effort** do we think might be involved in finding a solution?

The Impact/Effort matrix shown in Figure 8 is a frequently used way to help you map out the issues raised and identify whether the problem might be a quick win, a major project, a fill-in job or a thankless task.

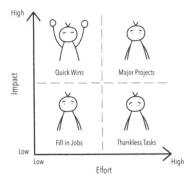

Figure 8 *Impact/Effort matrix*

Exploring the solution

Exploring solutions is designed to generate more than the usual suspects of ideas. It seeks to discover and increase your options beyond what you thought they were. This means that you can end up finding there are multiple options to choose from. This may feel like it is making your life harder, not easier. The more options you have, the more your anxiety might rise about finding the 'right' one.

You can get creative in looking for solutions. It can be fun or serious, but however you do it, stay with the process long enough to generate more ideas than just the usual suspects. Don't dismiss any of the ideas you have, as there is no such thing as a bad idea. Each one you consider might spin off into something else.

Ideation can be scary for some people; coming up with new ideas feels unachievable for them. Show you care, be vulnerable yourself and make sure you stick with Noticing, Acknowledging and Listening to them along the way.

Exploring with others

Why should you explore something with someone rather than simply telling them the answer or sending them away to work it out for themselves? Exploring takes time and energy. If you know the answer anyway, you may feel it is easier just to crack on with it. Sometimes this is indeed the case but exploring offers a host of benefits beyond simply the solution you may arrive at.

Here are three very good reasons to explore with others.

1. It is good for you personally.

   It helps you to **understand what the options are**; the other person may well have a different viewpoint to you. You will probably **learn** something as the other person may well have different knowledge to you. You may well **challenge** some of your preconceived ideas or biases, thus opening your eyes and broadening your view of the world. It may well expand your network and improve your **influence**. The other person's **engagement** arising from the process is also likely to have a positive impact across your department.

2. It is good for others and helps them to **learn.**

   It gives them **responsibility** and **empowers** them to make their own decisions. It is likely to **engage** them more effectively and help them be more **motivated** to make changes or take action. It includes them and helps them **feel valued**. It may well help them **see the bigger picture** and it encourages **generosity** and give and take.

3. Exploring something with a client, a boss or a stakeholder encourages **innovation and engagement.**

   They will bring a **different perspective**, a **diversity of thinking** to the topic. They will have more **buy in** to the final decision as it gives them the **ownership**.

> Actively seeking alternative views increases the
> **rigour of thinking** and is likely to improve the
> **final decision**. You will learn more about the
> **bigger picture**, which helps expand your **knowl-
> edge, experience** and **perspective**. The increased
> **connection** and active demonstration of **trust**
> and **value** for each other will improve your **social
> capital** and expand your **networks** and **influence.**

Imagine what a massive difference this could make to you, your team's culture and performance over time. Just look at the highlighted words.

If you are aware of them, you may like to use coaching models with other people to help them Explore solutions for themselves.[22] GROW (see below) is one of the classic techniques but there are many more to choose from.[23] If you use any of the coaching models, remember to NAL all the way through and they will take you nicely to Explore and Do.

It is always best for people to come up with their own solutions. Offering your own ideas should always be seen as a last resort. However, if someone is stuck, really has no ideas and really wants your advice or the benefit of your experience, always offer more than one option.

---

[22] Coaching is the art of asking the right questions to help an individual work through their own issues.

[23] Sir John Whitmore, *Coaching for Performance.*

G.R.O.W. Model, Whitmore

G = Goal

Example Question: What are we looking to achieve from this conversation?

R = Reality

Example Question: What is going on right now?

O = Options

Example Question: What options have you got?

W = Will

Example Question: What will you do next?

If you give just one idea it can come across as *the* answer, especially if you are in a position of power and influence. As you use NALED more, your influence will increase. People will trust you more and seek your opinion. If you are also their manager, your power over them increases. They'll take your answer and off they go.

You can frame your ideas in a story and use silly options to help unlock thinking (I often use aliens). Here are three options for you to try:

Option 1.

>'Can I tell you a story? I had a client/friend/colleague who was in a similar situation to you; they found two ways forward...'

Option 2.

>'I have thought of a couple of alternative ideas, can I share them with you?'

Option 3.

>'How about you jump on the next passing space-ship and hitchhike to planet Zog and leave it all behind? OK, here's another idea...'

Option 1 helps people see it from a different angle. Option 2 specifically asks their permission to help solve it and option 3 usually makes people smile and encourages fun and creativity.

Exploring your situation

Exploring together to avoid silo working

Exploring is good to do across departments. Many creative organizations will even bring in the customer to get their ideas when designing innovative products and services.

Getting the viewpoints and knowledge from different departments helps to solve things more effectively in the long term.

This is about generous sharing of knowledge. Where people are more generous with knowledge, it actively increases everyone's learning and creates more opportunities to improve, to innovate, to develop further.

Sir Tim Berners-Lee could have kept the internet for himself, sold it and made a lot of money. If he had, it wouldn't be what it is today. He didn't. He gave away this amazing free resource and ever-expanding network of information to the world.

When you protect your knowledge, you create silos.

Silo thinking and working is one of the biggest issues that organizations face – it's certainly one of the ones people come to me most with. Departments do not share information, explore together, communicate decisions. It creates wastage, logjams, poor investment decisions, misunderstandings and mistakes.

'I've seen this in action,' Diane from manufacturing told me, 'Our marketing and design teams came up with a new product. But they are based remotely from the factory and haven't asked us our opinion or talked to us. They think they know better.'

She went on to describe how, in this organization known for its creative and technical expertise, the remote location of the factory and head office had exacerbated a rift between the marketing/design team and the operational technical experts. Each were anxious to be proven right.

The head office marketing team had come up with a beautiful new product based on their research of the customer's changing needs. They invested in the product package design, the visuals and began to sell it to the customer.

Diane described what happened when the orders came in.

'We received the new packaging and the orders at the factory at about the same time. But there was a problem. The new packaging didn't fit the existing factory lines.' Diane was almost gleeful as she described the impact. 'All the packaging had to be scrapped and new packaging sent through. Their mistake in not talking to us meant that the customer got their order fulfilled late, the spec was slightly different and we wasted a lot of money on extra packaging.'

The silo working caused a major financial impact. If they'd explored the options together and shared their knowledge, this could have been avoided.

Actively seek diversity

Whenever you are exploring, remember that people are all biased in one way or another. Instinctively, humans create sense and meaning without being aware they are doing it. Don't pretend that somehow you are different, you are not! Below is a table of common cognitive biases. Take a look at it and note how many times that you have seen these in yourself and the people around you.

Examples of common cognitive bias

Anchoring bias	Loss aversion bias	Bandwagon effect
The first piece of information heard establishes the range of reasonable possibilities in each person's mind, e.g. in salary negotiation.	The pain of losing something is psychologically twice as powerful as the pleasure of gaining something. This can lead you to overplay the risk of losing and stay as you are.	The probability of you adopting a belief increases based on the number of people who hold that belief. This powerful form of groupthink is the reason why meetings are often unproductive.

Blind spot bias	Choice-supportive bias	Survivorship bias
Failing to recognize your own cognitive biases is a bias in itself. People notice cognitive and motivational bias more in others than in themselves.	When you make a choice, you'll feel positive about it, even if that choice has flaws.	You focus only on surviving examples, causing us to misjudge a situation (e.g. 'Being an entrepreneur is easy, I've not heard of any failures.').
Confirmation bias	**Judgement heuristic**	**Stereotyping**
You tend to listen only to information that confirms your preconceptions. You favour your own position; you know your choices intimately but don't fully understand others'.	You judge yourself on your intentions and blame external factors for getting it wrong; you judge others on their actions and character.	Anticipating a group or person to have certain qualities on small amounts of information. It allows you to quickly identify strangers as friends or enemies but people tend to overuse and abuse it.
Selective perception	**Outcome bias**	**Overconfidence**
Your emotions/ opinions influence how you perceive	You judge a decision based on the outcomes rather than how	Some people are too confident about their abilities, which causes

the world, e.g. You are more likely to spot transgressions in the opposing team than in our own when watching sports.	it was made in the moment. Just because you won lots in Vegas doesn't mean gambling was a smart decision.	them to take greater risks in daily lives. Experts are more prone to this bias than laypeople since they are more convinced they are right.
Zero risk bias People love certainty – even if it is counter-productive. Eliminating risk entirely means there is no chance of harm being caused.	**Pro-innovation bias** When a supporter of an innovation tends to overvalue its usefulness and undervalue limitations.	**Status quo trap** We prefer things as they are and tend to downplay the negatives of our present position rather than face the challenge of something new which may be worse.

In his quest for better results in 2020, England football manager Gareth Southgate challenged the natural bias and groupthink present within any team by actively seeking diverse views from outside the football world. This included national coaches from other sporting disciplines, senior military leaders, psychologists and even a leading sports journalist. At the time, he was criticized for this approach, which was a major departure from previous norms, but it was subsequently seen as pivotal in the improved culture and performance of the team in the following two major tournaments.

To challenge your biases and avoid groupthink, actively embrace diversity and challenge. Encourage input from people with expertise in alternative areas. Seek to challenge assumptions and traditions and systems. Ask 'How do we know?' and 'Why not?' Throughout all this, remember everyone has shortcomings in perception. Be kind.

Finally, remember that through the Explore process, you are seeking divergent thinking. You are seeking to open up your options, not close them down. This can make it feel overwhelming at times, so just remember that is what the D is here for. To help you decide, commit and Do.

Explore summary

- ✓ Explore the problem and the potential solutions.
    - ➢ Investigate a problem or issue to seek to uncover underlying issues.
    - ➢ Discover: come up with new solutions and alternative viewpoints.
- ✓ Remain curious to learn, share knowledge and empower others as well as come up with creative and innovative solutions.

✓ Explore both the big picture and the detail (think capital T).
✓ Keep using NAL all the way through the process.
✓ Remember the problem is likely to get bigger as you uncover more about it. That is OK.
✓ Actively seek diversity to avoid groupthink and yesterday's solutions to today's problems.

Chapter 7
Do

Do: to act or perform, to carry out, execute or implement, to behave, to proceed, to make.

Lena had a clear vision to 'level up' opportunities for young people in her region, but the issue was complex. She was stuck. Lena had come to coaching to figure out how to progress it. She wanted someone to help her see it from a different angle, to challenge her thinking and work out how to move forward. What should she do?

As we Explored her dilemma, we uncovered gaps in knowledge on the ground and wider political understanding. The move to Do proved simple. I asked Lena, 'Given our discussions and what we have explored now, what do you think are your next steps?'

Lena was immediately clear that she needed to know more about these gaps. She could not proceed without the additional information.

'I know what to do,' she told me. She had moved from being unsure and stuck to being confident and clear about how to drive this forward. She was on the phone in action within minutes of coming off our call, setting up a way to gather better knowledge.

The prompt to move to Do unlocked Lena's challenge and she suddenly felt again that her mission was possible.

Success comes from translating your dreams into reality. To achieve that, you have to do something; to take action to get you closer to your goals. Talking is all very well, but the proof is in the doing, in the action. That is where you truly progress.

Do is the decision, the commitment or the next steps. Do is where you get to move from talking to action; you move forward rather than staying inert.

- When you are using the NALED framework for your*self*, this strand is often the one that involves changing ingrained habits and patterns. It involves personal challenge.
- When you are using the NALED framework for *Others*, this strand helps them move forward and step into action.
- When you are using the NALED framework for a *Situation*, this strand is how you decide to advance together. It involves stepping up to challenge the status quo.

Stepping up to challenges and action can feel scary and hard though, which leads to the problem:

The problem: You often don't do

As Yoda famously says to Luke Skywalker in *Star Wars* as he was struggling to master new Jedi skills: 'Do or do not. There is no try.'[24]

---

[24] *Star Wars: The Empire Strikes Back.*

'I'll try' is often a cop-out. At best, you will only do something half-heartedly and give up at the first sign of a problem. To do effectively involves commitment, a resolve to follow through on an idea or a new course of action.

The question of when to move to this phase is one of timing. There are two traps to avoid: that of haste and that of inertia.

The trap of *haste* is where you jump to solutions mode too quickly, without fully understanding all the elements involved. By following NALE, this should be less of an issue. If you are prone to this trap, remember you don't have to get to the Do phase every time. Remember right back at the beginning, where my journey began with my husband? It was months before he was ready to do something about it.

The trap of *inertia* is where you fail to move to action fast enough. You may feel stuck or trapped; doing feels too hard, so you don't.

You may find you have a natural tendency towards haste or inertia, or that you vary depending on the situation. This chapter is for those times when you are stuck, when you don't do, to help you move away from inertia.

Humans in general tend to prefer things as they are and to downplay the negatives of their present position, saying 'it's not perfect but then what is?' (described as the status quo trap[25]). Humans are also primed to hang on to what they have; the loss aversion bias describes how the pain of losing

---

[25] First coined in 1988 by Samuelson and Zeckhauser.

something is psychologically twice as powerful as the pleasure of gaining. Inertia, or resistance to change, is therefore hardwired in to prompt you to remain as you are, rather than risk losing something through what you do.[26]

This is all well and good in relatively stable and predictable times, but in a changing, volatile world, doing nothing can be more risky than change.

> *'There are two traps to avoid: that of haste and that of inertia.'*

This problem of inertia can be even bigger in groups. You've all been in that meeting – often more than once a week. You talk about the issue, you have a good conversation but then... nothing happens.

Next week, you have a catch-up meeting and once again... nothing has happened. You all say the same things or talk about what you have done this week (or not done due to the number of ineffective meetings you've had) but there is no action, no 'oomph'. It can be demoralizing.

This is a pattern of behaviour I have seen many times. This kind of inertia can also be described as a fear of failure.

When the context is tough, challenging and there is no single right answer, making a decision or moving to action can be

---

[26] If you are interested in finding out more about cognitive bias and heuristics, we have included more information and links on the www.naled.org website.

a difficult decision. Leaving things as they are can feel like a better option.

At work this can show up as people putting up barriers to a potential solution, focusing on what will go wrong rather than what could go well or be learned.

It can also show up as people using delaying tactics, such as asking for more information, or passing decisions up the line. They'd often prefer to stick with what they know and hope the problem goes away than put themselves at risk by doing something.

When you step up to action, it can feel like you put yourself at risk. You are the one accountable for the decision. What if it goes wrong? What would that mean to me? What might the consequences of failure be? How might other people judge me? When you are accountable, this uncertainty causes anxiety and fear, which are powerful negative emotions.

To be fair, sometimes by waiting the problem can go away.

More often though, doing nothing often means that the problem gets worse, or the opportunity passes you by. Remember, 'it's the job that's never started as takes longest to finish.'[27]

The solution: Create the case for action

To overcome the natural human in-built resistance to change and committing to action requires motivation.

---

[27] Gaffer Gamgee's advice to Sam in the *Lord of the Rings.*

Sometimes the motivation comes in the form of a crisis, as in the shift to working from home and online meetings during the Covid pandemic. Usually though, creating the case is more complicated.

Motivation for change often happens when our **Resistance to Change** (RC) is less than the sum of our **Dissatisfaction** with our present position, **Vision** for how things could be different and the **Skills** or **Steps** to be able to make the change happen. This can be expressed in the form of an equation.[28]

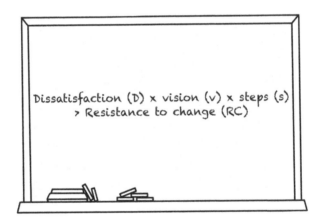

Dissatisfaction (D) x vision (v) x steps (s)
> Resistance to change (RC)

Figure 9 Beckhard-Harris Change Equation

If any of D, V or S scores zero or low, it's unlikely that you will commit to feel motivated enough to change. Building the case for action requires that you are dissatisfied enough, clear

---

[28] Commonly referred to as the Beckhard-Harris Change Equation.

enough, and skilled/confident of the steps enough to make the change happen.

You may find when you have moved through NALE effectively, the case for action will have been made. You will hear people say, 'I know what I am going to do', and your job is easy.

The NALED framework is flexible and you don't have to get to the Do phase, but it feels good when you do, especially where you have been discussing a specific issue or concern. It feels as if this is where the magic is happening; the action helps to unlock a previously stalled project, and it feels as if the universe has conspired to support you on the journey.

The act of making a decision or a commitment is **inspiring**; it gives us **hope**. A small act can set off an avalanche of positivity. By committing to something with someone, you become **invested** in their future. Suddenly, the relationship shifts; you become genuinely interested in the outcome. Getting to the point where someone feels comfortable enough to state their next steps and commit to them demonstrates **trust**. Trust forms the foundation of all relationships.

> *'A small act can set off an*
> *avalanche of positivity.'*

These are powerful words. **Inspiring, hope, invested, trust**. Creating the case for action and getting things done benefits you, others, your team and your organization.

How do you move to Do?

'If you always do what you've always done, you'll always get what you always got.' – Anon

The Explore phase is designed to create lots of ideas. It is divergent thinking with the aim of opening up understanding of the problem and generating ideas and options.

The Do phase is where we focus back down on a solution to test and try. It is convergent thinking with the aim of providing the focus and commitment to make choices and take action.

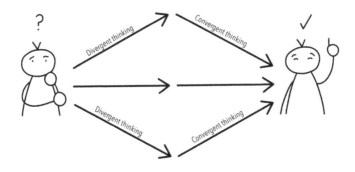

Figure 10 Divergent and convergent thinking

The move to Do involves four things: a decision, commitment, accountability and action. I'm going to take each of these areas in turn.

Making a decision

Whilst moving to a decision may feel natural and smooth, there will be times when you may struggle to narrow down your options to one solution or a few actions that you feel that you can commit to. The first step is to revisit your original goal, objectives or success criteria. Remembering what you are trying to achieve can help you identify the simplest next step.

Asking which idea to test first can also be helpful. This frames the decision as a hypothesis rather than the 'right answer'. Tests might not work first time round – this encourages intelligent failure (see below).

For people who like a more analytical approach, here are some simple tools:

- Try the impact/effort matrix introduced in the Explore chapter to identify quick wins.
- Try a voting approach for a team (if you give each person a nominal £100 and ask them all to 'invest' in the different ideas you will soon come up with a favoured one).
- Try forced ranking. (Pair up all the options against each other. Choose which idea you prefer out of each pair and give it one point. You then go with the option that scored the highest.)

When working with others who are struggling to decide, asking them what is their 'best guess' is often helpful. This moves it away from having to be the 'right' answer and allows them to bring their intuition to the decision-making process.

If you have limited time and need to move the conversation to a conclusion but are not sure whether they are ready to move on, I recommend being honest. Say something like: 'I have five minutes left, what would be the most helpful use of this time for you?' and if they are still unable to make a decision, arrange another time to continue the conversation.

Getting it wrong or intelligent failure

Getting it wrong is part of the learning process. Thomas Eddison was famed for saying: 'I didn't fail, I just found 5,000 ways not to do it.'

When you are seeking innovation or solutions to complex issues, getting it wrong is inevitable. Failure should be seen as an opportunity to learn. Your decision is unlikely to be perfect as there are rarely simple answers to complex questions.

In many organizations, failing is punished and so people don't try as hard. You get a 'zero failure' culture. To get more innovation, more critical thinking, more brains working on the job, it helps to instead encourage a culture of intelligent failure.

This is where decisions or actions are framed as a test, hypothesis or trial, rather than 'the' final answer. Trials are not expected to not work perfectly first time round, but give you essential intelligence on how to improve. This is especially helpful in complex, difficult or challenging situations. So, if for example you are breaking one of your own long-held habits, you might fail several times before you find the key for you. But by not succeeding first time round, you invariably find out more. Just remember to build in reflection time when you are testing so you can review, learn and continuously improve.

Commitment

Moving from decision to commitment is a small step but an important one. Often people will decide on a list of things they can do, which can feel unwieldy, too much and just never get started. I am sure you know someone who is great at writing lists, but never gets round to starting what's on them; I know a few...

One way you can support this commitment to action is to test how good the decisions or proposed actions are. The series of questions I often use look something like this:

1. Which of these actions feels like the most important for you right now?
2. How likely are you to do each of these out of 10?
3. What would make you grade them higher?

The first two questions help people prioritize actions and test their commitment to them. This helps to move you from a massive to-do list to maybe one or two actionable steps that really feel right to start with.

The third question, grading your likelihood of achieving something, helps you to be honest about how committed you are. Exploring what would make that grade higher helps tease out the support that might be needed or the culture/ systemic issues that might be holding you back.

Accountability

Once you have committed to and graded your actions, you will start to feel accountable for achieving them. Remember though, moving to action can feel scary.

Many people throughout their lives sit in the stands and watch the game playing out in front of them. They are too scared to step onto the pitch. They might be scared of failure and judgement. After all, if they have been judging others from the sidelines for years, it makes sense to assume others will judge them if they step up, right? Even the thought of success can be daunting, being thrown into the limelight and having to live with increased expectations.

By committing, by moving to action, by doing, you step onto the pitch, and you are asking others to do this too. It is not always easy. But it is usually important. As one of the managers I was recently working with remarked:

'At the end of our long strategy day, we all wanted to go to the bar, but you made us stick with it until we had agreed the next steps. That was the bit that made all the difference – we had to commit to something, move from thinking and ideation to action. By setting these down in stone and putting measurable elements against them, we could hold ourselves accountable for the actions. We all knew then what we were going to do and how we were going to take the business forward.'

The Do process is iterative. It requires you to follow it through, revisit it and check up on it. You need to make sure it does happen; otherwise people lose faith in themselves but, maybe more importantly, in you. If you say you are going to do something and then don't, you lose a little integrity. Integrity is one of the foundation stones of trust. You really don't want to risk that.

When you feel accountable for something, you are more likely to achieve it, which is why weight loss is easier when you do it with other people, why KPIs are used in business and is one of the reasons that coaching is so successful for performance improvement.

Here are a few questions which help to create accountability. I am sure you can think of more:

1. When will you do it by?
2. What would you like me to ask you next time I see you?
3. How will we know this has happened?

You can do this for yourself. Make yourself accountable by identifying a buddy, a coach or ask team members to check up on you.

Taking action: Tiny Little Changes (TLCs):

'A journey of a thousand miles must begin with a single step.'
– Lao-Tzu

Actions create reactions, which builds momentum. When you start to roll a snowball down a hill, it takes quite a lot of pushing to get it moving, but once it is, it has a life of its own. This can be how it feels when you start to agree together to act and change things.

It's important not to make the actions too hard, or too diffi-cult. Keep it real and keep it small. Better to achieve one small step forward than to do nothing because the action was just too hard. Use the acronym TLCs, Tiny Little Changes. Each tiny change put together can make a massive difference over time. Many single steps put together complete a marathon.

Look at Captain Sir Tom Moore, the man who walked around his garden during the 2020 lockdown to raise money in the run-up to his 100th birthday on a walking frame. It was an amazing act that he achieved one step at a time. His actions also sparked a cascade of similar 'heroic' fundraising activities.

Scott Doolan became the first paraplegic to reach Everest Base Camp in 2018. Despite his wheelchair breaking, he walked on his hands to get there. He talks about every step being agony, but each step being one further to his goal.

Your goals may not be so bold, courageous or well known; however, every step takes you closer to achieving positive change.

> *'Every step takes you closer to achieving positive change.'*

What to watch out for

Taking it back

When working with others, it's really easy at this stage to ask, 'How can I help you?' and end up with a big 'to-do' list back on your desk. The trick here is to make sure that the ownership of the action or decision lies in the right place.

If you are a helpful person in general, you are likely to take on actions to oblige. This can be counter-productive in the long run and take people's self-agency away from them. When you have helped someone come to their own decision about what to do, then keep on empowering them; don't take it away from them now.

Instead of trying to 'help', give away the power, the responsibility and the ownership of the action. It might not be what you would do but that is OK.

Do summary

- ✓ The move to Do is where you step up and challenge the status quo; it can feel scary and may not happen quickly.
- ✓ The biggest risks to successfully doing are haste (too fast) and inertia (too slow), but this is a balancing act.
- ✓ Creating the case for change involves ensuring that your steps, vision of the future and level of dissatisfaction are greater than your resistance to change.
- ✓ The move to this phase can feel natural; however, there are times we need help, or need to help others to build the case for action.
- ✓ Doing involves making a decision, having commitment, accountability and moving to action.
- ✓ Making changes and moving to action can feel hard, but by taking it one step at a time we can move mountains.

Chapter 8
Applying NALED in a nutshell

Practice: *to perform something repeatedly in order to acquire or polish a skill, to make a habit of.*

I have run through the full framework in great detail. The likelihood is that I have given you so much information that you won't know where to start.

On top of which, I know you are a hugely busy person with a massive to-do list. You've got a tough job.

Firstly, here is a summary of why this is important.

Your tough job is unlikely to get any easier as our world gets more complex.	The most likely derailer of your work is human relationships and human bias.
Getting better at understanding yourself, understanding others and understanding the world around you will make you more likely to succeed and might even make your job easier.	You are already using NALED when you are at your best. You can be at your best more often by intentionally using this framework.

I am going to run through how you apply NALED in the real world, in a busy working life, so that you can build in practice simply and easily.

You may have long periods of time to sit down with each of your team and truly use NALED with them. If you do, you absolutely can use it in that way, and I know you will see great changes.

However, if like most people you don't have that time available, then weaving in the different strands of NALED in five-minute bursts on a regular basis is likely to be just as effective in the long term in developing strong relationships and boosting performance.

I've given you a framework which you can use flexibly to get better outcomes. You can choose to use it in three ways:

1. Choose to have a different kind of conversation.
2. Choose to show up and respond differently.
3. Choose to see the world differently.

You make these choices every time you interact with those around you – whether on a video call, email, in a meeting, on site, in the office or in a formal setting. Create a foundation for yourself, starting slowly. Knowing and doing are two different things and if you do want to change things, take it one step at a time.

> *'Knowing and doing are*
> *two different things.'*

Each of these choices is a shift in how you do things; it takes a conscious effort to start with. I'm going to run through each of these briefly and outline how you might approach the challenges they might throw up for you along the way.

Choice 1 – Choose to have a different kind of conversation

Choosing to use NALED to have a different kind of conversation disrupts the patterns that you have got into over the years. Using NALED with others, in our interactions with them, can change our worlds one conversation at a time. I've seen it happen; it happened to me.

I've told you about a couple of times when the relationship with my partner was dysfunctional and ultimately was only going one way. Downhill. One conversation at a time, I chose to do it differently, to Notice, Acknowledge and Listen rather than try to fix him. Over time, it made a massive shift. Our relationship is stronger.

I told you too about the relationship between business development and marketing in one of my former roles. We both had different ideas about what the function of our departments should be, and the conversations always went one way – badly! 'Your job, no it's your job, no yours…' Again, it wasn't until I chose to have a different conversation with the marketing people that we began to make progress. One conversation at a time the relationship opened up and the stalemate was resolved.

Choosing to have a different kind of conversation will help you become more socially aware. You'll start to become more aware of patterns, of how to approach things differently and the impact you have. Many people choose to start testing NALED at home before taking it into work.

I recently took my own advice and practised having a different conversation at home.

My teenage son and I had been arguing rather a lot recently (for rather a lot, read all the time). We argued about everything. He would do nothing and yet expect me to clean up after him. It was 'so unfair' if I asked him to do anything.

So, I might just have shouted, often my default position. I know it's hard to imagine that I am not completely perfect in every way, after all I teach how to strengthen relationships and move through difficult conversations. Gah!

After too many days of fighting, I had had enough. There had to be another way. So, I stopped, noticed how I was showing up, and the impact this was having on the situation. I took a deep breath, became a grown-up, apologized for setting him a bad example and promised to try harder. I acknowledged I had a part to play in the situation.

He smiled at me (for the first time in a while), said thank you and said he would try harder too!

It worked because I had truly put aside my parental frustrations and spoken to him without laying my emotions on him. I had non-judgementally acknowledged my part in the problem.

The following day was loads better. And the one after that. The relationship shifted from being stuck in that pattern.

Do you have a relationship that has been soured by background frustrations and emotions? You could try putting them aside, apologizing and seeing what happens. Or not. Your choice. You can choose to hold a different conversation.

A good place to look to have a different conversation is when you have a catch-up with your colleagues. Try having a five-minute check-in with your teammates. It doesn't take long to have a meaningful conversation.

NALED in five minutes

If you are in a projects or operations role, it is likely that you have many issues arising every day. This simple framework of NALED questions will transform how you engage with the people around you to tackle these issues.

It includes some simple phrases to use, but these are just to start. Find your own way of phrasing that feels right and comfortable.

Title	Sample questions	Thinking behind it
The Opener:	Tell me what is on your mind? Or: What would you like to talk about?	Keep it open, show you are interested. Demonstrate you care.
The Digger:	What is behind this?	You are Noticing and Acknowledging their issue and Listening, all at the same time.
Dig Deeper:	Anything else?	As above, you are showing curiosity and acknowledging there might be other things behind it.
The Explorer:	What do you want to do with it?	Explore but put the onus on them.
The Action:	What needs to happen next?	Give the ownership of the solution over to them and wrap up the conversation.

Choice 2 – Choose to show up and respond differently

'Between stimulus and response there is a space. In that space is our power to choose our response. In our response lies our growth and our freedom.' Stephen Covey writes of Victor Frankl's teachings.[29]

---

[29] Stephen Covey, *The 7 Habits of Highly Effective People.*

The philosopher Victor Frankl discovered the power of choosing your response whilst being a prisoner in a Nazi concentration camp during the Second World War. He realized you always have a choice about how you respond in any situation. Using NALED by yourself helps you to navigate that gap between stimulus and response. By Noticing and Acknowledging the cognitive biases, the patterns, the deep-seated beliefs you have, you move away from automatic responses to choice. This choice gives you freedom and the ability to bring about change.

Choosing how you show up helps you to develop better emotional intelligence, to become more self-aware and hence to become more resourceful through effective self-management.

How we show up creates our reality. Let me share an example of this.

Mick rose through the ranks to become a senior operations manager through his ability to solve problems. He is another person who makes things happen, who fixes things for people. People loved him. He made it easy for them to call him to fix things for them. He cared for them, and he wanted to help them.

He became so good at fixing stuff that people brought more and more things for him to fix, and before he knew it, they couldn't fix things for themselves anymore. He travelled the country fixing stuff. Sorting out problems.

People brought him so many problems to fix, there were not enough hours in the day. He worked all hours. His health suffered and his home relationships too. Mick cared, and deeply, but his desire to fix things for people nearly destroyed him.

As he began to understand the impact of his behaviour, he realized that he needed to show up differently. He started to push back and encourage people to solve their own issues. But by this stage it was almost too late. They expected a quick fix, not to be taught how to do it for themselves. He had created his own hell.

Mick ended up leaving the job, as this was the only way he could see to break the pattern. It took him some time to recover and find the right role and the right approach, but now he practises helping other people to solve their own problems and is far more effective.

My best self

Here is an exercise I have found useful in helping people to explore how they want to show up.

Draw a line down the page. On one side put 'me at my best' and on the other put 'me at my worst'. Then be honest. How do you show up and respond when you are at your best, and what about when you are at your worst?

Here is an example for me:

Figure 11 The best and worst me

One project engineer who recently completed this exercise made a laminated copy of his list to keep in his pocket. He shared with me that before every meeting he quickly referred to his list to remind himself who he was at his best and that this was how he wanted to show up to this meeting.

Choice 3 – Choose to see the world differently

Your first choice was about your social intelligence: how you interact and connect with others. Your second choice was about your emotional intelligence: how you regulate yourself. This third choice is about your situational awareness: how you respond to the world around you.

You can use NALED on the world around you to spot opportunities and threats.

The first part is to Notice and Acknowledge the bigger picture. If we don't notice, we can't do anything about it.

There is a classic urban myth about boiling a frog. Apparently, if you try to put a frog into hot water it will jump out.[30] Put it in cold water and slowly heat it through, it will not notice and will slowly be cooked. True or not, it illustrates a principle: we are often unaware of subtle but constant changes in the world around us. Unless we actively notice our environment, it could slowly be the death of us.

There are many stories of this happening in business: Kodak cornered the market for developing photographs until the digital camera came along. They didn't notice how big the trend was becoming until their market all but disappeared. Nobody

---

[30] I don't recommend testing this out.

wanted the hassle of sending off films to be developed when we could go digital and see them instantaneously. Ironically, Kodak even designed the first digital camera but decided to sit on it, selling the patents for how to do it to others.

Nokia and Blackberry were similar. They both held the market share in mobile phones until the next generation of phones came along. They didn't notice, or failed to acknowledge, the contextual change in the market inspired by innovations like the smartphone.

Sometimes change is faster paced. Let's think about the last few months of 2020. High street retail giants started tumbling as the slow move towards online shopping accelerated through the coronavirus lockdown. As more people had to shop online, they realized how easy it was.

Consider working from home – before the pandemic, it was considered 'lazy'? Now it seems likely that hybrid working will be a core part of our working lives for the foreseeable future. Did your organization notice and adapt? What impact did that have on how people felt about working there?

Disney noticed that the biggest problem for people visiting their theme parks were the queues to pay for things. So, they designed a creative solution – payment wristbands, and the queues disappeared. Not only did the queues disappear but people spent more. Hurrah!

The context around us changes constantly. Using NALED combined with classic business models, such as PESTLE (Political, Economic, Social, Technology, Legislative, Environmental), Porter's Five Forces[31] model, and stakeholder analysis are powerful ways to explore and respond to the world in which you operate.[32]

What are you Noticing? What are we Acknowledging and, more importantly, what are you not acknowledging as a business? Who are you Listening to and, more importantly who should you be listening to? What should you be Exploring? Is there an elephant in the room? And, what do you need to Do to ensure that you remain relevant and competitive in our world?

Again, let me share with you an example of this in action.

---

[31] Michael Porter, *Competitive Strategy*.
[32] These and other resources from the book are available online at www.naled.org

Rob is an engineering manager; he told me his story of how he had applied NALED at a situational level.

There was a stand-off between his and another department, with each blaming the other. Nobody was talking; in fact, they were so annoyed that they wouldn't even visit each other's offices. The job had stalled because each department was too proud to address it.

After learning about NALED, Rob chose to try and see his world differently. He approached the other head of department without judgement. He said, 'I notice this has stalled' and simply asked what the issue was (Notice, Acknowledge, Listen). He was informed about a lack of paperwork and asked more questions. It turned out when they explored it together, that all they needed to do was sign their project sheet. Five minutes and it was all sorted out.

'I had been really nervous about doing this before,' said Rob, 'but having the framework made me confident that I could handle pretty much anything they would throw at me, I knew where to go. As it turned out, they didn't throw anything at me, probably because I went in without a pre-judgement.'

'So, it's all sorted now?' I asked.

'Yes, the project is back on track. It was costing the organization for each day of delay. By facing up to that one conversation, I have straight away saved them money and saved the project. It felt really good *and* it was easy to do.'

'What would you do next time?' I asked him.

'I'd have that conversation straight away.' He said, 'To be honest I feel a little silly for being so fearful of having it. Now, I am confident that I know how to cope with whatever they can throw at me. I'm just quiet, I hold back my emotional response and I listen to find out what they think the problem is, so that then we can come to a mutual solution.'

Summary

- ✓ Applying NALED effectively takes practice.
- ✓ You can use it in three different ways to help improve your soft skills.
    - ➢ You can choose to hold a different kind of conversation.
    - ➢ You can choose to show up and respond differently.
    - ➢ You can choose to see the world differently.
- ✓ Practising NALED only needs five minutes to be powerful.

Chapter 8½

STOP and reflect

Reflection: *the process by which you gain insight into your professional practice by thinking analytically about it.*

The process of learning is never ending. To get better at soft skills, it is important to continuously reflect to both celebrate your progress and help you identify where to prioritize next.

In this chapter are two suggestions of ways in which you might reflect on a regular basis to evaluate your skills and progress. You will find:

1. A questionnaire to evaluate your soft skills so you can understand how you are improving.	2. A way to reflect on the quality of your relationships and where to focus attention

Questionnaire: How good are your soft skills?

Soft skills can be seen as the sum of your ability in three key areas:

1.   How self-aware and self-managed you are (emotional intelligence);
2.   How you communicate and engage with others (social intelligence); and
3.   How you see the world (situational awareness and openness).

Here is a questionnaire for you to answer that gives you an idea of how you are performing in each of these areas. I suggest doing it now to get yourself a baseline figure, then repeating the questionnaire in four to six months to evaluate progress.

Don't think too hard, and don't try and game the system – this is only for you, so be honest.

Area	Question	DATE: Score out of 5
Emotional Intelligence	I recognize that I have emotions running at all times	
	I am aware of how these emotions impact my thinking/reactions	
	I can usually name which emotions I am feeling	
	I quickly recover my equilibrium after feeling strong emotions	
	I am aware that I am seeing the world through my biased lens	
	I can regulate my emotions well	
Social Intelligence	I can usually sense the emotions of others	
	I am comfortable with their strong emotions	
	I can change my approach with others to build relationships even when emotions are running high	
	I listen before I speak most of the time	
	People trust me easily	

	People are comfortable to tell me what is really going on for them	
	I ask people rather than tell them most of the time	
	I respond rather than react to people	
Situational Awareness	I actively seek to understand the bigger picture	
	I actively seek to understand what biases and assumptions might be at play	
	I seek to uncover the real issues before jumping to solutions and advice	
	I can see when the system is causing issues rather than individual people or parts	
	I actively seek to be challenged in my thinking	
	I look for people that see the world differently to me to get a fuller picture	
	TOTAL	

Add up the total of all your responses and write it here: ... /100

Score 0–40

You have some work to do. You probably already know this. It is likely that you are unaware of the impact that your emotions have on those around you and your ability to see the world. It may also be the case that you don't think that you have many emotions (spoiler: you do). You are, however, self-aware enough to have scored yourself low so you might actually be better at this than you think. You have the potential to lift your performance, your relationships and to make your life easier by making a few simple changes. Read on.

Score 41–80

Most people will probably fit into this category. Sometimes you get it right; sometimes you don't. You probably have some work to do. Mostly, you are pretty well regulated but you have blind spots and these are likely to be causing you some issues. You know you are a work in progress and that is fantastic.

Score 81–100

You are either pretty awesome at this or the opposite. Hopefully, you are self-aware enough to know that you have been working on yourself for many years and have honestly self-evaluated to get to this level. The alternative is that you think you have all this stuff sorted but don't know what you don't know. Yet. That is also OK; the first step is to be aware of it.

Taking the questionnaire twice:

Note: You may well find that your scores actively go down once you are more aware of yourself and the more you practice. That is OK.

'The more I know, the more I realize I don't know,' said Albert Einstein, and this is the definition of wisdom. The more you become aware, the more you will realize when you could have done it better. This awareness is the first stage of learning.

Reflection: How good are your relationships?

How easy is it to maintain good relationships with those around you? At home, how easy are your long-term relationships with your parents, friends, partners, siblings, children? How good is your communication with them?

At work, how about those with your teams, managers, stakeholders, suppliers, customers and peers? How robust and resilient are those relationships? How much do you trust one another, or feel as if you have (and give) strong leadership – not management (getting the job done) but leadership (getting people to get the job done)?

This is primarily a book for business, for relationships at work. However, the principles contained within it work equally well at home.

Your social capital is the sum of the quality of your relationships with stakeholders (i.e. anyone with a vested interest in your organization): be they customers, suppliers, owners, staff team, regulators, your local community, leaders, your family and so on. Here is a way to measure it.

Get yourself a piece of paper.

Draw a picture of
yourself in the middle.
Like this:

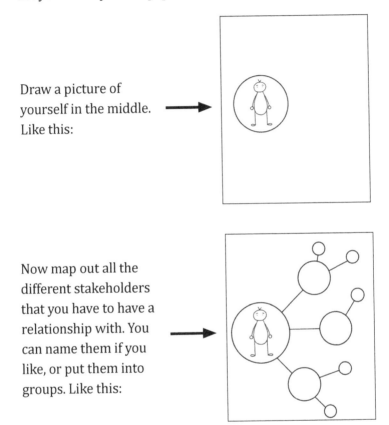

Now map out all the
different stakeholders
that you have to have a
relationship with. You
can name them if you
like, or put them into
groups. Like this:

Once you have done this, I want you to consider your relationship with each of these. Give it a mark out of 10 as to how good it is. If you mark them at 0 it means you don't know them at all. 10 would be a really strong relationship (robust, reliable and resilient, as discussed above). Your gut feel is fine for this exercise. This is for you so be honest with yourself.

Once you have put a number against all of them, consider where you think the relationship should be, given their importance in your work and home life. For example, if you are wanting to get the senior leadership's buy-in for a new idea, you might need to have stronger relationships and greater influence within this team. If your team are facing a challenging project you might want to lean in with them. Take a different coloured pen and, once again, mark them out of 10 as to where they need to be for you right now.

Which relationships have the greatest difference between where they are and where they should be? These are the ones you need to work on.

Simple!

OK, so now you have it clear where you need to prioritize your attention as you improve and strengthen your relationships.

Chapter 9

Challenges you might face

'Smooth seas do not make skillful sailors.'

African proverb

I recommend you come back to this section of the book when you are listening more intently and begin to come across some issues. Below are a few of the common issues and challenges you might come across as you start to listen and hear people more.

This is normal and shows you are challenging your 'usual chat' to do things differently.

Here is a selection of different approaches to specific challenges you might face.

What about when the conversations get tough?

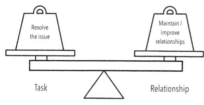

Figure 12 The balance between task and relationship

There will always be people who challenge us, who think differently, with whom we clash, but you still need to maintain effective relationships so that you can work as a team, influence them, engage them and manage and lead them.

There is a balance to be struck between getting the job done and developing strong relationships. This is what delivers more effective teamwork.[33] Too much on the task side and

---

[33] There is lots of research on this subject, a good start point is *Effective Teamwork* by Michael A West.

you face team burnout pretty fast. Too much on the relationship side and nothing gets done.

In your career, you will have to hold people to account as you maintain this balance between tasks and relationships. It is in these times of conflict, challenge and difficulty that our soft skills and relationships are truly tested.

It's easy to consider the soft skills when you have time, when the relationship is good, and when you are specifically thinking about having a NALED conversation. But when things are tough, or challenging, how do you approach it?

Here is an outline of how to approach a formal or difficult conversation in a way that pulls together all the different things discussed so far and some of those yet to be covered.

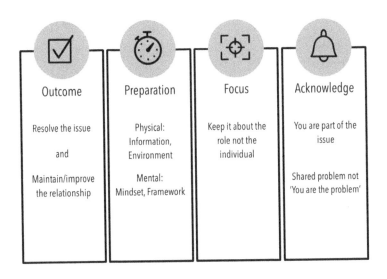

Outcome	Preparation	Focus	Acknowledge
Resolve the issue and Maintain/improve the relationship	Physical: Information, Environment Mental: Mindset, Framework	Keep it about the role not the individual	You are part of the issue Shared problem not 'You are the problem'

Outcome: As Stephen Covey would say, 'Begin with the end in mind.'[34] The successful outcome for a challenging conversation is both solving the problem and, at the very least, maintaining the relationship, but ideally improving it. If, in how you solve the problem, you damage the relationship, all you will do is create further problems for yourself in the future. Remember this.

Prepare: Think about physical and mental preparation both for you and for them. Physically consider the environment, the timing, information and administration. Mentally consider mindset, attention and what framework you might use.

Focus: Keep it about the role that that person performs – not about them. When it gets personal, the gloves come off.

Acknowledge: Acknowledge your part in the problem; for better or worse you are a part of this. Position the conversation as a shared issue to which you are seeking a shared solution.

Maintaining this balance is not easy, but doing so will both get the job done and give you an engaged and happy team.

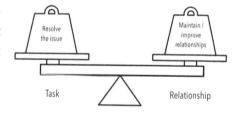

---

[34] Habit number two from *The 7 Habits of Highly Effective People* by Stephen Covey.

What about when my buttons have been pushed?

How you respond when someone tells you something that pushes your buttons matters. How do you respond when they make a mistake that has implications, when they raise concerns that you don't want to hear, when they come up with an idea that is a shocker, when they question you or tell you that your 'baby is ugly'?

In these moments, it helps to remember three simple things:

1. Respond with gratitude

   Say 'thank you' for bringing an issue to your attention or for the idea they have shared. This gives you time to think. It is polite and encourages them to keep bringing things forward. The last thing you want to do is to stop people speaking up!

2. Respond with curiosity

   Use NALED to find out more. What's behind the issue? How did you come to that idea? What other ideas do you have?

3. Respond with feedback

   Not everything is gold, so you shouldn't treat it as such. Help people to understand what was good or what the bigger picture is so that they can contribute more effectively in the future.

Watch out though. Watch out for your biases, for your opinions and judgements or patterns of behaviour with that person. Have you pre-judged them? There may be 99 shocking ideas before you get one good one.

How do I turn down the level of emotion?

Sometimes in formal, challenging conversations, the level of emotion can rise.

There are things you can do to power up and power down a conversation, so if you have managed to self-regulate enough to stay calm, here are some things you can do to keep emotions in check.

Firstly, remember your responses – those on the left of the diagram will power up, or escalate the emotion, fast. Those on the right will help power it down, or de-escalate. Choose which response you are going to have.

Secondly, remember another simple acronym: MRI – Most Respectful Interpretation.

It is easy and very human to judge others harshly. You tend to judge yourself based on your intent but you tend to judge others based on their character – 'they must be awful people, that is why they just cut me up at the traffic lights...'

If you can try and remember to consider the Most Respectful Interpretation of any given situation, it will help you not to pre-judge people harshly, but rather think the best of them until proven otherwise. Give it a go. It feels good and it gets positive results.

Negativity breeds negativity. Put a halt to it by engaging in MRI.

Thirdly, remember to use *Name it to tame it.* I've already mentioned this tip in the Acknowledge chapter, but it is powerful. By naming the emotions that you and others feel, you can begin to regulate them.

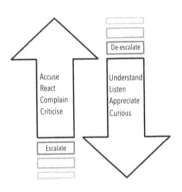

Figure 13 Turning down the level of emotion

What else should I look out for?

This chapter is not meant to scare you, but it would be disingenuous of me not to tell you what to watch out for. Listening is awesome, but as with anything that encourages people to be open, it has risks and a personal cost. It's tiring, it's harder work than not listening, and it can lead us down weird paths we didn't expect. But get it right and I think that you will find it to be amongst the most rewarding experiences you have had.

Boundaries

It is important that you create boundaries for any NALED conversation to protect yourself.

You will find a surprising number of people who are experiencing levels of anxiety, sadness or other strong emotions that has tipped over into a diagnosable condition. **It is not your job to diagnose or treat this**. Care, compassion and listening are the best things you can give someone as a non-medical person. But you should be very clear about the boundary of mental illness, which marks the point where you need to step back from the conversation and signpost more qualified support.

People may seek to pull you into their dramas. **You are not a counsellor or therapist**. If you are using NALED, this does not mean you take responsibility for someone's wellbeing – it just means you have a tool with which to hold a difficult emotional conversation. Watch out for the line. Watch out for getting sucked into a psychological game such as the Drama Triangle[35] we explored in the Acknowledge chapter. You might want to help, but you may well not be the best person to do so.

---

[35] See Chapter 4 for more information.

People will presume that there is a **boundary of confidentiality**. As we have explored, trust is paramount in any relationship and in the successful application of NALED. Nobody will welcome people sharing what they have said without explicit prior agreement. There may be times when something is shared which you can't keep confidential, such as something illegal or an issue of safety. If this does happen, you may need to stop the conversation and let the other person know that this information can't be kept confidential and must be shared with the appropriate authority.

I have some **physical boundaries** too; some people, particularly in the male dominated organizations in which I work, seek to dominate or influence using their physicality. You can use the environment to help calm this (e.g. have a table between you or meet in a public space). Often this is a pattern which you can disrupt, but it does take time.

You also need to set **boundaries for your time**. Whilst you will want to make yourself available, you also need time for yourself. Some people love to talk and it's hard to shut them up. When you know this, set a time limit and be open about using it: for example, 'We've got ten minutes, what would you like to achieve in this time?'

Whenever possible, be clear about your boundaries before entering a conversation and share these with the other person upfront. If you haven't done this at the outset and during the course of the conversation you start to become uncomfortable about the direction it is going, be courageous, Acknowledge and Listen to your sense of unease, pause the conversation and reset the boundaries.

It's not always easy. You'll have to learn what your boundaries are. If you want some standard coaching ethics as a guideline for where these should be, you could try one of the coaching professional bodies;[36] they have strict and mutually agreed Codes of Ethics regarding some of these boundaries.

Tears

These can make us feel uncomfortable. But they are important.

> A Polish lady I was working with told me that 'I can't bear the English – they are always trying to give me tissues if I cry. I am crying because it is important – don't tell me to wipe them away, I am proud of those tears!' I found this challenging, as someone from a very middle-England background where tears are a sign of weakness and not OK. Today, I am much more accepting of tears and find them easier to navigate. They are important. Don't ignore them. Don't apologize for them.

Patterns/language

Most of us are locked into certain patterns of behaviour (including me and you, I assure you). Learning how to

---

[36] Association for Coaching (AC), International Coaching Federation (ICF), European Mentoring and Coaching Council (EMCC) are a few you can find in the UK.

spot them helps us decide if we want to change them. I've mentioned this a bit already, but you may start to notice that certain conversations always go certain ways. Acknowledge this pattern as it might not be helping you.

Language is powerful; how you phrase things matters; your pitch, tone and body language also matter. I've already mentioned not using the word 'Why' as it is loaded with emotion. Keep an eye on how you phrase questions; you might find it is unhelpful. Equally, in a team situation you might find that having a shared language is helpful with your relationship building. Exploring a tool like NALED together can give you a shared language and be very helpful.

People with whom nothing works

It's important to recognize when a relationship has moved into the toxic phase; when it's gone beyond redemption. I know in my life there are a few relationships that I have decided not to continue. There are people with psychopathic, manipulative or narcissistic personality traits. The bottom line is, if you feel bad or drained of energy as a result of your relationship with another person, it's time to sit down and assess the issue. You can't change them; you can only change yourself or your situation. If you make a decision to limit your time with this person or end the relationship, don't look back.

The benefits of support networks – who do you talk with?

As a qualified coach, I have other coaches and a supervisor that I talk with on a regular basis to offload, work through problems and to develop my own practice. It is a really good idea if you are starting to work on NALED in your organization that you have someone who can support you and talk things through with. This might be a group or someone independent who understands what you are seeking to do. Professional bodies, as detailed above, have supervision groups that you can join. You will often also find local coaching peer groups. Many people are willing to practise their skills and get into co-coaching relationships with one another.

Next steps

If you enjoy listening and want to do more of it then I recommend tooling yourself up through research, training and co-coaching support. NALED is a simple introduction to some of these things. You might find as you start to do it more, you become interested in one or more of the following areas and wish to take it further. I've included reference materials on the www.naled.org website. Also, I regularly update and send newsletters out with useful things I and others have come across. You might like to start looking for materials around the following topics:

- Coaching conversations
- Emotional and social intelligence
- Vulnerability
- Psychological safety
- Teamwork
- Leadership
- Motivation
- Transactional analysis

Chapter 10

Stories from the front line

Stories: accounts of incidents or events, facts pertinent to a situation in question, news articles, anecdotes.

Below are some stories of how NALED has had an impact both at an organizational or group level to change behaviours and culture, and at an individual level to impact on daily lives.

Group stories

I've been teaching and practising NALED with groups of people across different industries for three years now. Here are some of the areas in which it has been used in practice.

Developing trust and psychological safety[37]

A global construction company team had been working on a project with a long, difficult history and a short contract future. Relationships had been strained. The senior leader was looking to shift conversations on site from being compliance and task based to being more in depth and human focused. By doing this, we intended to build trust and psychological safety, to uncover hidden issues and to encourage ideas and questions.

We introduced the NALED framework across different levels of the organization. This was done during the coronavirus lockdowns, so delivered online. It was tough. Soft skills for construction managers is never easy to deliver, but doing it online during tough times was even harder.

---

[37] For a description of psychological safety, see Chapter 2.

Yet they engaged. The NALED conversations encouraged people to get to know one another in a different way. They then became more curious and wanted to hear more. They began to see the impact of showing up to a conversation differently and being able to choose how they responded. It gave them new skills that many of them tested out at home to build relationships there as well as in the workplace.

By using NALED to demonstrate care, develop relationships and deepen interpersonal connections, the people helped build trust, improve psychological safety and improve the flow of information.

'On the back of this initiative, I consciously decided to deploy the techniques whilst we delivered a project. I took a slight step back, gave more oversight and refused to be the man in everyone's face and driving them to exhaustion/frustration. That sounds easy but actually it was very hard to start off with; I had to make a real conscious effort to hold myself back multiple times. I watched more, I listened more, I supported the team more and do you know what? I actually believe I added more.' *David*

Entrepreneurial thinking

We worked with a series of teams of engineers looking to step up and actively try new things in their organization, where the organizational culture actively discourages risk. We used NALED in three ways with these teams to help them embed the core elements of the learning programme.

We used NALED to help with situational awareness because to be more entrepreneurial you need to spot opportunities; you need to see the world differently. You can try this next time you conduct a SWOT analysis (Strengths, Weaknesses, Opportunities, Threats). Try using NALED at the same time and see what else comes up for you.

We used NALED to develop the individuals, to challenge assumptions and biases, hear alternative viewpoints in order to find new and innovative ways forward in relation to the complex challenges they were facing. It helped prevent echo chambers[38] and unlock creative solutions.

We used NALED to develop social capital because when you are trying something new and taking risks, you'll need support. If your relationships are strong, you feel able to stretch them by persuading and influencing people to follow or go with you, and to support you when things don't go to plan. They could identify the relevant stakeholders and actively decide where to focus their attention.

The results were spectacular. The engineers became more proactive, more confident, with better collaboration and engagement, and improved stakeholder relationships.

---

[38] See the story about Gareth Southgate in the Explore chapter for more on echo chambers.

We began to see a cultural shift from 'tell' to 'ask' in their departments.

> 'I've noticed as a team this course has made quite a shift in how we work. We are making a conscious effort to think differently and step up.' Mark

Improving engagement

A global manufacturing organization was having issues with communication and engagement following a significant number of operational and personnel changes.

The HR manager told me: 'The communication is just not right. When we talk about communication, they think we mean whether they give information by email or over the phone... there is just no awareness of social intelligence. I think they are nervous of how to approach each other.'

We ran a series of workshops, introducing NALED to help the operational, manufacturing and product teams interact more effectively. We started with the operations team.

This team had been working together for many years – some of them had been in the organization for 30 years. They knew each other pretty well. They had fallen into patterns of conversations and often pre-judged each other's responses.

Through encouraging them to actively Notice, Acknowledge and Listen to one another before they moved into the Explore and Do-ing stages, they learned how to re-examine and redis-cover themselves and each other. Conversations moved from being transactional to transformational. Blocks were uncov-ered and dealt with, opportunities discovered, challenges faced head-on.

> One particular manager recognized that his usual way of 'bawling out' poor performance was actively working against him and managed to turn around his personal patterns. It has made a huge difference in engagement within his team.

Collaboration

We were working with a project team that had been brought together to deliver a short-term, fast-paced and pressur-ized project. They needed to accelerate the team-bonding process and move to collaboration quickly.

The experience of learning NALED and practising together encouraged the building of trust, allowed them to be honest and open, gave them a shared language and vision of how the relationships could be, and, probably most importantly, a method of approaching difficult conversations that undoubt-edly would be coming given the level of pressure on their project.

The team decided to actively measure the team relationship over the course of the project and check in with each other using NALED on a regular basis. It made a big difference. They were truly able to collaborate, bringing all their ideas to the table, challenging assumptions and testing and stretching themselves to deliver the best possible project.

The project took place in the heart of the coronavirus pandemic, when anxiety and uncertainty were running high, when changes to rules were happening daily. The project still succeeded to deliver a good product and developed more collaborative relationships with other teams across the organization. The team cited their conscious efforts to develop social capital through deliberate NALED conversations as a key success factor.

Final thoughts

Not every conversation is right to be a NALED conversation. There is, of course, space for chat, discussion and banter. If you used NALED all the time, you would not only be exhausted but probably come across a bit intense.

Hopefully this has given you a framework with which you can become more intentional in those moments when it matters.

Finally – good luck. You have a tough job. But developing your soft skills should make it a bit easier in the long run.

Remember you are already doing this when you are at your best. Just get a little bit more intentional or slightly better, one conversation at a time.

I hope you enjoy the journey. I know I have.

Discover

online tools and resources at

www.naled.org.

Bibliography

Beckhard, R. & Harris, R., 1987. *Organisational Transitions: Managing Complex Change.* Addison-Wesley.

Bolton, G. & Delderfield, R., 2000. *Reflective Practice: Writing and Professional Development.* SAGE.

Bungay Stanier, M., 2020. *The Advice Trap: Be Humble, Stay Curious and Change the Way You Lead Forever.* Page Two Books.

Covey, S., 1988. *The 7 Habits of Higly Effective People: Powerful Lessons in Personal Change.* Free Press.

Damasio, A., 1995. *Descartes' Error: Emotion, Reason and the Human Brain.* Harpperen.

Edmondson, A., 2018. *The Fearless Organisation: Creating Psychological Safety in the Workplace for Learning, Innovation and Growth.* Wiley.

Eisenberger, N. & Cole, S., 2012. Social Neuroscience and Health: Neurophysiological Mechanisms Linking Social Ties with Physical Health. *Nature*, 15, pp. 669–674.

Google, n.d. *Re:Work with Google.* [Online] Available at: https://rework.withgoogle.com/print/guides/57213 12655835136/[Accessed November 2021].

Ishikawa, K., 1968. *Guide to Quality Control.* JUSE.

Jobs, S., 2011. *Steve Jobs: His Own Words and Wisdom.* Cupertino Silicon Valley Press.

Karpman, S. B., 2014. *A Game Free Life.* Drama Triangle Publications.

Kaushik, A., 2007. *Web Analytics: An Hour a Day.* Sybex.

Markowsky, G., n.d. Physiology. *Encyclopaedia Britannica.* [Online] Available at: www.britannica.com/science/infor-mation-theory/Physiology [Accessed June 2021].

McGregor, D., 1960. *The Human Side of Enterprise.* McGraw-Hill.

Navarro, J., 2008. *What Every BODY is Saying: An Ex-FBI Agent's Guide to Spead-Reading People.* HarperCollins.

Porter, M., 1998. *Competitive Strategy: Techniques for Analysing Industries and Competitors.* Free Press.

Samuelson, W. & Zeckhauser, R., 1988. Status Quo Bias in Decision Making. *Journal of Risk and Uncertainty*, 1, pp. 5–59.

Siegel, D., 2011. *The Whole-Brain Child: 12 Revolutionary Strategies to Nurture Your Child's Developing Mind, Survive Everyday Parenting Struggles, and Help Your Family Thrive.* Delacorte Press.

Sinek, S., 2019. *The Infinite Game.* Portfolio.

Star Wars: Episode V - The Empire Strikes Back. 1980. [Film] Directed by George Lucas. Lucasfilm Ltd.

Tolkein, J. R. R., 1955. *The Lord of the Rings.* Houghton Mifflin Harcourt.

Torre, J. & Lieberman, M., 2018. Putting Feelings Into Words: Affect Labeling as Implicit Emotion Regulation. *Emotion Review*, 10(2), pp. 116–124.

West, M. A., 2012. *Effective Teamwork: Practical Lessons from Organisational Research.* 3rd ed. BPS Blackwell.

Whitmore, J., 2002. *Coaching for Performance: GROWing Human Potential and Purpose.* Nicholas Brealey Publishing.

Index

A

accountability, notion of 155–157
acknowledge
    of emotions 58–63, 76
    of facts to yourself 63
    of good, the bad and the ugly 56–57
    methods to
        acknowledging others 67–70
        acknowledging self 61–66
    Name it to tame it technique 70
    non-verbally 68–70
    our situation 72–75
    of problem 56–57
    of self, other(s) and the situation 17, 56–57
    of solution 57–58
    of tough situation 58
    verbal 67–68
    watching out
        with others 75–76
        for yourself 75
    of your biases 64–66
Acknowledge, Check, Expand (ACE) 74–75
    application of 75
action and reaction, dynamics of 35
active listening 84

advice monsters 99

B

bad, acknowledging of 57–58
Bandwagon effect **137**
Beckhard-Harris change equation *149*
Berners-Lee, Tim 135
bias 35, 48
    acknowledging your 64–66
    anchoring **137**
    Bandwagon effect **137**
    blind spot **138**
    choice-supportive **138**
    cognitive **137–139**
    confirmation 124, **138**
    judgement heuristic **138**
    loss aversion **137**, 146
    outcome **138–139**
    pro-innovation **139**
    survivorship **138**
    zero risk **139**
body language 38–39, 92
    dance as 95
Bungay-Stanier, Michael 99
business development 54

C

commitment to action 154–155
confidentiality, boundary of 193

confirmation bias 124
conversation
    acknowledgement of 188
    focus on 188
    getting tough 186–188
    NALED 187
    outcome 188
    preparation for 188
    quality of 7
    responding with
        curiosity 189
        feedback 189–190
        gratitude 189
Covey, Stephen 85, 167, 188
critical thinking 154
curiosity
    for learning 98
    responding with 189

D
Damasio, Antonio 59
dance
    as body language 95
    listen to 95–96
Dave's story 60–61
decision making 9, 28, 110,
    152–153
discomfort points, for noticing 46
dissatisfaction 149
doing, importance of 18–19
    accountability 155–157
    case for action 148–150
    commitment to action
        154–155
    decision-making 152–153
    divergent and convergent
        thinking 151
    Do phase 151, 156

getting it wrong 153–154
impact/effort matrix 152
intelligent failure and 153–154
the problem 145–148
the solution 148–150
taking action 157–158
taking it back 158–159
traps to avoid 147–148
drama
    Drama Triangle (Stephen
        Karpman) 77
    sympathy and 77–78

E
echo chambers 74, 121
Edmondson, Amy 89n14
effective communication,
    approach for 39
effective listening
    distraction to 91–92
    principle of 91
Elliott, case study of 59
emotional intelligence 35, 59, 171,
    179
emotions
    acknowledging of 58–61
        Name it to tame it method
            for 70
    emotional outpourings 76
    turning down the level of
        190–191
entrepreneurial thinking 201–203
exploring
    5-Whys 127–128
    to actively seek diversity 137
    to avoid silo working 134–137
    common cognitive bias
        137–139

Fishbone Diagram 127
Impact/Effort matrix 129, *129*
importance of 18
with others 121–122,
    130–134
our situation 122, 134–137
the problem 117–120
    key stages 125–129
reasons for 121–122
for self 121
the solution 130
solution to 120–121
strategies for 122–125

F
feedback, responding with
    189–190
Fishbone Diagram 127
Ford, Henry 87
four bums on a bench (WWWWH)
    96
Frankl, Victor 167–168

G
good, acknowledging of 57
Google's 2016 Project Aristotle
    89n14
gratitude, responding with 189
group stories
    collaboration 204–205
    for developing trust and
        psychological safety
        200–201
    entrepreneurial thinking
        201–203
    for improving engagement
        203–204

groupthink 74, 140
G.R.O.W. Model 132, 133

H
haste, trap of 146
Highest Paid Person's Opinion
    (HIPPO) effect 74
hope, importance of 150

I
Impact/Effort matrix 129, *129*,
    152
inertia, trap of 146–147
information, interpretation of 32
innovation and engagement 131
inspiring, importance of 150
intelligent failure, culture of
    153–154
Intentional Loop 6, **7**
interpersonal risk taking 89n14
invested, importance of 150

J
Jan's story 82–83
Jobs, Steve 58

K
Karpman, Stephen *77*
key performance indicators (KPIs)
    73, 156

L
language, as tool to communicate
    93
leadership 93–94
    development of 5
    qualities of 58

Lean methodologies 127n21
learning
    curiosity for 98
    patterns of 194–195
    process of 178
Lena's story 144
listening. *See also* effective
    listening; silence
    active 84
    check to ensure understanding
        102
    compassion and
        demonstration of care
            88–89
    to the dance 95–96
    for deeper understanding
        89–90
    distraction to effective
        listening 91
    driven by your own agenda
        84–86
    effect on thinking 90
    empowerment due to 89
    good listening 86–87
    importance of 17–18
    intention to 92
    to the music 94–95
    principles of
        asking simple open
            questions 96–98
        be fully present 91–96
        remaining curious for
            longer 98–101
    problem regarding 84–86
    reasons for 87–88
    skills 84
    solution of 86–87
    as superpower 83–84

    to the wider voices 98
    to the words 93–94
    to your inner voice 98
    to yourself 102–103

M

McGregor's Theory X and Theory
    Y 50
mental wellbeing 112
Moore, Tom 158
Most Respectful Interpretation
    (MRI) 190–191
motivation, theory on 50
music, listen to 94–95

N

Name it to tame it technique. 70
natural break, between NAL and
    ED 110–112
non-verbal acknowledgement
    68–70
non-verbal communication 69
Notice, Acknowledge, Listen,
    Explore, Do (NALED)
    framework 8–11, 51, 68, 95,
    110, 120, 124, 129, 133, 145,
    150, 162, 200, 202
    application of 193
    boundaries for 192
    choosing to
        see the world differently
            171–175
        show up and respond
            167–169
        use 164–166
    for developing social capital
        202
    five strands of 15–19, *19*

my best self 169–170
people with whom nothing
     works 195
principles of
     authenticity 20
     enjoy the messiness 19–20
     taking small steps 20–21
notice/noticing 25
     actions for increasing
          effectiveness of 30–41
          noticing people what they
               say and how they are
               saying it 36–39
          others 36–39
          self 30–36
          situation 39–41
     concept of 16–17
     core areas of **29**
     discomfort points 46
     exercise in noticing 41–47
     importance of 34–35
     intentional 27–29
     interpretation of information 32
     the problem 26–27
     solution 27–28
     things to watch out for
          focusing on the negative
               48–49
          seeing what you expect to
               see 49–50
     what you find easy 47–48

O
online training programmes 128

P
patterns of behaviour 194–195
perception, selective **138–139**

perfect leader, image of 93
Philippa's story 71–72
physical boundaries 193
Political, Economic, Social,
     Technology, Legislative,
     Environmental (PESTLE) 173
Porter's Five Forces model 173
problem
     defined 127
     noticing of 26–27
     worksheet 125, **126**
problem solving 87, 99, 116, 118
     skills for 2
     systematic approach to
          120–121
psychological safety 88, 89n14,
     200–201
public space 193

R
Reactive Loop 6
relationship, importance of 35
Resistance to Change (RC) 149

S
self-awareness 35
self-fulfilling prophecies 50
Self, Other and Situation (SOS)
     acknowledging of 56–57, 61
     interconnectedness of 14, *14*,
          29, 47
self-starters 50
Siegel, Dan 70
silence 91
     as tool for listening 100
Sinek, Simon 88–89
situational awareness **180**
social capital 132

use of NALED to develop 202
social intelligence 59, **179–180**
social media 124
'soft' skills of relationships 9, 16, 178–180
Southgate, Gareth 139, 202n38
Star Trek 58
status quo trap **139**
stereotyping, issue of **138**
strategic thinking 7, 8
support networks, benefits of 196
SWOT (Strengths, Weaknesses, Opportunities, Threats) analysis 202
sympathy 77–78
systematic thinking 125

T
task and relationship, balance between *186*, *188*
tears, importance of 194
thinking, divergent and convergent 151

thinking, keeping the other person doing 98–99
time, boundaries for 193
Tiny Little Changes (TLCs) 157–158
Toyoda, Sakichi 127n21
trust, in relationship 150

U
ugly, acknowledging of 57–58

V
verbal acknowledgement 67–68
voice, tone of 38

W
words, listen to 93–94

Z
'zero failure' culture 154